QUIT "GOING" TO CHURCH...

...And Other Musings of a Former Institutional Man

By

STEVEN L. ROGERS

Copyright © 2007 by Steven L. Rogers

QUIT "GOING" TO CHURCH...
by Steven L. Rogers

Printed in the United States of America

ISBN 978-1-60266-176-9

All rights reserved solely by the author. The author guarantees all contents are original and do not infringe upon the legal rights of any other person or work. No part of this book may be reproduced in any form without the permission of the author. The views expressed in this book are not necessarily those of the publisher.

Unless otherwise indicated, Bible quotations are taken from the *New International Version* (NIV). Copyright © 1984 by International Bible Society.

All Rights Reserved
Steven Rogers
Norwalk, Iowa
U.S.A.

www.xulonpress.com

QUIT "GOING" TO CHURCH...

...And Other Musings of a Former Institutional Man

TABLE OF CONTENTS

FOREWARD... ix

INTRODUCTION xiii

1 GRANDPA..17

2 INSTITUTIONAL MAN 21

3 GOOD NEWS?..37

4 THE B-I-B-L-E...45

5 WHAT'S WRONG WITH THIS PICTURE?..............55

6 BLACK CAT 63

7 DISCIPLINE FOR THE "HELL" OF IT.....................71

8 MINISTERS 81

9 CHURCH CONSUMERS 91

10	HAZARDOUS MOBILITY 99
11	I'VE BEEN WONDERING 107
12	TO "HELL" AND BACK 119
13	MONSTERS IN THE CLOSET 129
14	A DISTANT LIGHT 137
15	THE CONCLUSION IS INCLUSION 145
	APPENDIX 153

ACKNOWLEDGEMENTS

It was a particularly meaningful and heartwarming experience for me to focus upon the people who directly influenced and assisted me in the writing of this book. They are special people who have in a variety of intended and unintended ways flavored every word I have written. I consider each one to be a gift from God. These are the people who have provided much of the *community* I have mentioned we all need in this book. They have taught me, advised me, prayed with me, had fun with me, scolded me, disagreed with me, put me in my place, encouraged me, worried about me and, most importantly loved me. And I love them more than I've been able to properly express.

To my brilliant, beautiful, creative, and thought (and otherwise) stimulating life companion, Sally, who inspired in me the courage to unleash what she saw in my heart and go for the dream; to my incredible parents who never gave up on me, set the bar for Christ-likeness, offer support, and mentor me in so many ways; to Erik and Amanda, our son and daughter, and Tanya and Ian their spouses who help me think cross-generationally and cross-culturally and have given us some exceptional grandkids; to Dr. John and Jennifer Dilley who provided invaluable content and editorial assistance with the manuscript and with whom I've shared friendship since high school; to Gregg, my brother and hunting buddy, and his wife, JoDee, who model how to be like Jesus without a bunch of religious baggage; to Tom Clegg, who introduced me to the writing of Brian McLaren and at strategic points in my life, usually over coffee, has given me paradigm changing resources for re-thinking my Christianity; to Furman Conard whose "spurs" and friendship I've appreciated since junior high; to Jim Beaird, friend, former denominational colleague and confidant who for some reason still hangs with me; to Pastor Michael Hurst with whom I have breakfast every Monday morning, from whom I've learned so much about the evils of exclusion, and whose congregation resembles what it will be like in heaven when every kindred and tribe is assembled in God's presence; and to Glen (Clothman) and Rhonda Moyer who dared to see something in us that we hadn't yet seen in ourselves, drew us into their circle of friends, and taught us that the best place to encounter Jesus is in transparent, simply structured, loving relationships; I can only say thanks, I love you. You sculpted this book in me.

FOREWARD

The best-selling author, M. Scott Peck, tells us that, "...virtually all of the evil in this world is committed by people who are absolutely certain they know what they are doing..." (From the Forward to *A Question of Values* by Hunter Lewis). This is an extremely sobering thought, especially when a reader decides to explore a new author whose content is of a religious nature. The dilemma in picking up such a book is in knowing whether or not the "certainty" of the author represents seeds of evil or fertilizers of faith. The former can unknowingly impregnate our thinking and ultimately our behavior, while the latter can stimulate an authentic, vulnerable and growing faith perspective. I suspect that some readers who come from within the traditional Christian church might wonder about this author's words due to the rethinking of some central beliefs that it may require, while those outside the church may feel a curious interest in his probing challenge to "hold our beliefs with an open hand." In both cases, this book has much to say to all of us wanting and needing a better understanding of the theme of inclusion, which is at the center of the Christian message and at the heart of this book.

Steven L. Rogers reminds us in a personal, user-friendly and compelling way, that we are all members of a universal neighborhood; and if we are to survive, then inclusion based on a fundamental respect of persons must permeate our thinking and actions reflecting our global relationships. Too often the stronger one believes, the more exclusive the club. One's theology becomes the result of mere intellectual assent to a relatively complicated creed and adherence to a prescribed pattern of behaviors. Compliance is then mistaken for conviction, and what one believes becomes predominately what distinguishes and separates one from others.

A winsome welcome awaits you in this Mr. Rogers' neighborhood. You will especially love his game of Black Cat, as well as the description of his confusion and utter exhaustion while functioning as a bodyguard for a famous evangelist when she came to his town. The refreshing and frank disclosures will help you appreciate the perspective he now celebrates, both because of and in spite of his life experiences. The implications of his thoughts about the 'church outside of the church' and 'redemptive lift' are profound and contagious. He grapples fluently and consciously with issues that many of us have been spoon-fed to uncritically trust; and his proclamation that the real good news of the gospel is of a heaven all will enjoy is certainly contrary to the segregationist theology within and without the major world religions. As our planet shrinks, that which distinguishes us is more vivid, and the potential for friction based on differing core beliefs becomes monumental and potentially catastrophic. If a movement toward inclusion doesn't occur now, then when? How much closer to pervasive provincial prejudice must we get before our real beliefs yield a more gracious heart toward our neighbor? We are all now living in a world that suffers from information overload, as Alvin Toffler warned of in his 1970 *Future Shock*, so it's a legitimate question to wonder if the following pages are worth the time and the energy to read. The answer is a wholehearted *yes*. Although there is nothing "absolutely certain" in this book, it's likely your faith will somehow grow by reading it. You can trust this author....I did and I still do.

Dr. John B. Dilley, Clinical Psychologist
West Des Moines, IA, USA

INTRODUCTION

A common thread connects each of the stories and accompanying applications you are about to read in the upcoming chapters. One by one, they tell of the many and varied ways I have personally, as a product of traditional, institutional, fundamental, evangelical, Pentecostal Christianity, both practiced and been on the receiving end of *exclusion*—seeing oneself or one's group as having superior beliefs, preferred standing with God, and holding to qualities and ideals that distinguish us from others.

Exclusion of people and ideas contrary to our own was at the heart of the rigid biblical dogmatism I learned at an early age. It's a worldview that understands God to have taken out on his own beloved son, Jesus Christ, his wrath over our sin, and, who continues to be full of rage, ready to deal similarly with each of us who doesn't toe the mark. You'll walk with me on a path of judgmental and exclusive arrogance that flavored various "soulwinning" and recruiting tactics I learned and employed to get people into my church. I'll share my realization of how the "us vs. them" nature of my once-held orthodoxies breeds quarreling and strife—yes, exclusion—between competing 'Christian' groups.

Please know in advance that I harbor absolutely no ill will toward those who passed down to me the only Christianity they knew. I do not question for a moment the genuineness of their faith or sincerity of their motivations; they deeply desired, and still desire, to please God. Many of them have made astounding personal sacrifices to take the gospel to remote and dangerous places in the hope that God would use them to rescue "perishing" souls.

But as I take a careful look at our world today, it has become increasingly difficult for me to reconcile the *exclusion* of others I was taught with the *inclusive* nature of Christ's message I have since discovered in my own study of the Scriptures and spiritual journey. Along the way, some things simply weren't adding up for me. A "witness for Christ" that heaps shame and condemnation on others doesn't seem to align with the Jesus who came to rid the world of shame and condemnation. A 'Christian' agenda that groups people into classifications that draw sharp boundaries between those who are "saved" and those who are "lost" is foreign to what Jesus modeled and taught in the New Testament. An "Americanized" version of Christianity that produces a power-wielding, militaristic swagger that obscures the compassion and servanthood Jesus so emphasized is very troubling indeed. When we just shrug our shoulders and give tacit approval to racism, something is very wrong. When consumerism and materialism are flaunted as virtue and defended as evidence of God's favor, while the ranks of the economically disadvantaged are swelling, something isn't right. When some Christians write off most of the world's population as deservedly doomed, while they secretly celebrate every new disaster headline as evidence their 'ticket out of here' will soon be punched, it's a disgrace.

For me, a desire to be "right with God", combined with fear, doubt, guilt, spiritual ambiguity, and growing cynicism, became the soil from which grew deep theological questions over the years. The search for answers to these questions has led to a change of mind as I have given myself permission to rethink some of the assumptions I so leaned upon entering into adult life and career ministry. Drawing upon experiences as a son, brother, student, husband, father, pastor, missionary, church planter, and denominational position-holder, I offer these still emerging changes in and from my point of view.

The purpose of this book is three-fold. First, it's a call for believers in Jesus Christ to commit ourselves *en masse* to making this a better world by feeding the hungry, helping the poor, clothing the naked, liberating the oppressed, loving our neighbors, striving to be peacemakers, and even smiling once in awhile—false piety that masks itself behind dour expressions, stern legalism, and cloistered irrelevance must become a thing of the past. It's a call for us to make it a better world by incorporating spiritual disciplines like worship, prayer, meditation, stewardship, servanthood, and community into a holistic lifestyle that makes no distinction between the secular and the sacred. Let's stop merely "going" to church and concentrate rather on *being* the Church in day to day life.

Second, and perhaps more importantly, this book is an invitation to those who have been turned off by what they've seen of Christianity, and have yet to discover God's amazing grace that has been extended to us through Jesus Christ, to take a fresh look at it through a new lens.

And finally, what I have written here is an apology of sorts for my own lack of understanding and compassion which may have somehow prevented someone from getting to know how loved, accepted and reconciled to God (and each other) we truly are because Jesus came and lived among us for awhile.

I seek to add my voice to the growing ranks of those who are rethinking what it means to be a follower of Jesus Christ in the 21st Century. Please take my hand and travel along on my journey, and we'll reconsider together the *"old, old story of Jesus and his love."*

1

GRANDPA

The Lord is not slow in keeping his promise, as some understand slowness. He is patient with you, not wanting anyone to perish, but everyone to come to repentance.

2 Peter 3:9

I'm not sure where my journey to inclusion began. It was like a sunrise overtaking a full moon night. At what point did the moon glow give way to the sunlight? Gradually shadow yields to shade. It's a process. All I can say is I now see things in a different light than I used to. My mind has been changed.

Perhaps the seed of change was sown in that first prayer request I learned as the pastor's toddler son in that little Pentecostal church where we prayed for "unsaved loved ones." There was one such loved one my family prayed for more than any others. Whether it was because he was the most 'unsaved' of all, or just the one we felt the closest to is hard to say, but it was Grandpa Rogers on whom we focused our prayers. I loved my Grandpa. To me, he was what manhood was all about – a perfect blend of Lucky Strike cigarette smoke, bibbed overalls, perspiration and Old Spice. Grandpa took me rabbit hunting and fishing. Grandpa had a TV when we didn't. Grandpa kidded around and teased us kids. Grandpa bought me my first bicycle. According to family folklore, he was the toughest man around and never lost a bar fight. He was a giant in my childhood, my hero.

But Grandpa smoked and drank and didn't go to church with Grandma. That meant, as *we* were taught to believe, he was a sinner headed for an eternity in hell. Of course, as a young boy I couldn't grasp the full implications of that, but I knew it was something I didn't want for my Grandpa. So I prayed earnestly for Grandpa to "get saved". As I look back on it, I'm not sure whether I was hoping God would come on the scene and make Grandpa give up his bad habits and start going to church, or whether I was hoping Grandpa would figure out he'd make God and all of us happy if he'd start living the 'good Christian' life. Either way was fine with me so long as we all could breathe a sigh of relief knowing Grandpa was one of us – the saved.

Hell-fire and damnation sermons were frequently preached in my church and were always followed by an emotional appeal for repentant sinners to come forward to the altar and give their hearts to Jesus. As I grew old enough to have an elementary understanding of sin and its wages, these sermons left me with two prevailing sentiments. The first was a strong feeling of guilt about my own waywardness. There were some ugly sins in my life, even as a grade school boy. Hardly a week went by that I didn't disobey my parents, fail to tell the truth, get into a fight with my brother, and experiment with every new cuss word I was learning. So by the time those red-faced, spit-spraying, angrily shouting preachers would finish describing the wrath of God and painting word pictures of the horrors of hell, I couldn't wait to get out of my seat and get to the altar to ask for God's mercy and get my sins washed away by the blood of Jesus—again. But my second sentiment was always to wish Grandpa had heard that sermon. Surely if he had, he would have gotten saved. So on the one hand I'd be grateful for another chance to get right with God myself, and at the same time be worried that Grandpa had missed his chance.

There were many sermons about "the Rapture"[1] and the return of Christ in our church. It was one of the main incentives to keep us from going to movies and playing cards. "What if Jesus came back while you were doing that?" they would threaten. It was a scary thought for a long time in my childhood until I got old enough to figure out that if Jesus delayed his return until after I'd been to the altar on Sunday night, but before school on Monday, I'd be set to be taken up in the Rapture and wouldn't have to do the homework my teachers had assigned for the weekend. From about sixth grade on, I hated waking up on Mondays because the Rapture hadn't occurred in the night and I still had all that homework to get done before class. I got in the habit of putting off getting saved again until Sunday nights, too. Of course, if Jesus had decided to come get us on Saturday, instead of after I'd been to altar at the Sunday Evening Evangelistic Service, I'd have been toast! Certainly, after a week at school with my peers and the mischief we'd get into on Friday nights, I had neither the right garments for the Marriage Supper of the Lamb[2] or any 'oil for my lamp'.[3] And, as I had learned from all those hell-fire and brimstone sermons, you don't want to be in that condition when Jesus shows up... you could end up weeping and gnashing your teeth! I was counting on those Sunday evenings at the altar to get me re-outfitted for holiness, along with the other backsliders and 'lukewarmers' that seemed to make up a sizeable portion of the congregation. Sure, it was a gamble, but after all those passing weeks and years when he didn't come; the odds seemed in my favor. And the weekends, at least Fridays and Saturdays, were more fun that way.

One thing I wanted to believe through my immature worldview was that Jesus was stalling his return because he was waiting for Grandpa to get ready. I couldn't imagine enjoying heaven with Grandpa not there, or with a God that would leave him behind.

Grandpa died a number of years ago, having first discovered he was included in God's reconciling embrace of grace through Jesus Christ. He didn't go to church but he did go to heaven.

2

INSTITUTIONAL MAN

~

"Do you ever think you'll get out of here?" ...

"One day, when I've got a long white beard and two or three marbles rolling around in my head, they'll let me out. ... I don't think I could make it on the outside, Andy. I been in here most of my life. I'm an institutional man now..."

Conversation between Andy Dufrain and Red in the *Shawshank Redemption*, Warner Bros. Pictures

Most of my role models and mentors were in *it*. They are great men and women of faith, integrity and a spirituality I continue to admire. My own father, the foremost of all my mentors, served *it* in a key leadership capacity for several decades. Many family conversations through my youth and on into the present have centered on the current events and policies of *it*. From *it* I received an education, a career path and substantial sums of support money for various ministry assignments my wife and I accepted in *its* name. Invitations to serve on *its* boards and policy-making bodies started me on the climb up *its* leadership ladder. For more than thirty years *it* shaped my belief system and governed every career decision. In exchange for all of this, my wife and I gladly contributed to *it* more than ten percent of our annual income year after year. When our kids reached college age we urged them to pick *its* school. *It* has been the true north of my spiritual compass, my primary source of fellowship and the definer of my significance. Then, one day I discovered that, like Red in the *Shawshank Redemption*, in *it* I had become an institutional man, walled into an existence that found me unprepared to function on the outside. *It* is a denomination and there are many denominations.

I want the reader to know that what I'm about to express is not out of any ill will toward the heritage from which I come. The denomination in which I grew up and was affiliated with for so many years has treated me well and I owe it sincere gratitude. Any frustration I express is not directed at any denominationally- affiliated person. If any blame is to be assigned, it must be directed toward me since the decision to be a denominational man was my own.

Here is how it happened. Growing up as a pastor's son in the tumultuous 1960's, I resisted the mold into which the church had tried to press me as I proceeded through my teenage years. I went the way of most of my peers into the world of the counter-culture. We were down on the "establishment" and protested against a society that didn't seem to want to "give peace a chance". I went away to a state university and quit going to church.

Like so many others of that time, I experienced the emptiness of the drug culture—the lows get to be much lower than the highs. We were a confused and angry generation who had thrown off restraint, only to find the kind of "freedom" that leads only to a dead end where one finds oneself with nothing left to lose.

Then came the Jesus Movement. It was a "radical" new way to practice the old time religion. One could have long hair and wear hippie clothes and be a Jesus freak. Far out! Traditional church folks didn't like it, which made it all the more appealing to us. When the Jesus Movement arrived in my hometown, only one pastor and local church that I know of made any effort to build relationships with these new Jesus freaks. The young pastor would open the basement of his home every Friday night to have "rap sessions" about God.

In an altered state of mind and looking for something to do, I, along with several of my friends, staggered into that pastor's basement one October evening. Cigarette smoke was thick in the room and some of the words being used were definitely not the kind of words one usually heard in church. But, as different ones spoke of finding Jesus and having a personal relationship with him, I felt something I had never felt before in the churches where I was the preacher's kid. It was raw. It was real. It was God, and I wanted more of it! Sitting cross-legged on the floor I mumbled a simple prayer. "If this is you, God, this is what I'm looking for."

What happened next was a miracle—that's the only way I know how to explain it. Instantly I was clear-headed and completely sober. All effects of the drugs I'd been using daily for months and all day that day vanished as if someone had flipped a switch. Since that day, I have not used an illicit drug or been intoxicated by any substance. Say what you will about the immaturity and excesses of the Jesus Movement, it was the exit ramp from the highway to destruction for me.

I quit using drugs and started reading the Bible. A few days later I was overtaken by a strong desire to go to Bible college and, conveniently, there was one near where I lived that was affiliated with the denomination in which I had grown up. As a son of a one of their ministers, I was given a 50% discount to enroll there. It seemed like the best option.

Meanwhile, I continued to attend the nondenominational church across town where the Jesus Movement was happening. Dozens of hippies, some barefooted, crowded into the front rows each Sunday. Word spread. I spread it at the Bible college. Students began to leave the churches that were denominationally affiliated with the Bible college to check out this "happening" church.

Pastors and parents from these denominational churches were alarmed. Not only was that "independent" church across town letting long-haired hippies without shoes come into their sanctuary, they didn't even teach all the same doctrines the Bible college taught! It was decided that something had to be done. Local denominational pastors, faculty and school board members huddled together to solve this troubling development. The ruling was handed down that students enrolled in this denominationally sponsored Bible college must attend an approved sponsoring church or be expelled from school. With great reluctance, and only because I was highly motivated to get that Bible college degree, I complied. The institutional doors clanged shut behind me as I left the church where Jesus "was moving" to attend a church the denomination insisted I attend. Gradually I embraced life on the inside and devoted an entire career to succeeding in the denomination—an institutional man.

Amazingly, other than telling his disciples they had more to learn than he had told them, and offering vague reassurance that the Holy Spirit would lead them along the way into the rest of the truth (John 16:12-13), Jesus left no instructions as to how his followers were to organize themselves.[1] His commandment to them was simply to love God wholeheartedly, love one another and spread the good news. Apparently, Jesus expected that if his followers would live in loving relationship with God, their neighbors and themselves, his overall mission of taking the gospel into all creation would be accomplished.

After Jesus left them, and as they were still reeling from all the events that had surrounded their involvement with Jesus of Nazareth over the course of the previous three years, the apostles and the little band of 120 Christ-followers waited prayerfully in Jerusalem for whatever was supposed to happen next. Peter evidently spent some time studying the Psalms and concluded from portions he lifted out of two different ones (Psalm 69:25 and Psalm 109:8) that they were supposed to appoint someone to fill Judas' place among the twelve apostles. The lot fell to Matthias.[2] This was the first recorded organizational action of the early Christians.[3]

Shortly thereafter the little group of Jesus' followers experienced a spiritual power encounter that dramatically altered the course of their lives and human history. When a crowd gathered to investigate the commotion, Peter stood up with the other apostles and explained that what they were observing was the fulfillment of what the Jewish prophet Joel had prophesied. Joel had apocalyptically[4] foretold of a time coming when there would be universal change in the established order of things that would have global consequences and be participated in by young and old, male and female (Acts 2:17-21).[5] Peter then segued into the Jesus story and encouraged them to change their minds about Jesus of Nazareth. *"God has made this Jesus, whom you crucified, both Lord and Christ,"* he declared. These were troubling words to a crowd made up of worshippers assembled in Jerusalem from all over the Mediterranean region that had come to worship at the temple. Someone in the crowd shouted up to Peter, "If this Jesus, who was crucified by the Romans at the behest of some of our religious leaders just fifty days ago, is, in fact, Lord and Christ, as you're proclaiming, what must we do?" To which Peter replied, "Change your mind about who Jesus is (repent) and be baptized in his name for the remission of your sins, and you'll, too, experience being filled with the Spirit." Three thousand did.

Perhaps it would be helpful to define some of the terms I'm using before proceeding too far in this discussion. An often-used term is *institutional*. Institutionalization happens when organizations make the *preservation* of the systems and functions they had designed to accomplish their mission more important than the actual completion of their mission. *Institutional Christianity*, therefore, tends to place greater priority upon maintaining structures, roles and traditions instead of accomplishing Christ's mission.

Another term that is used with frequency is *organized* or *organization*. I use these words in reference to the various ways any group of people working together establish communication, protocols, and structures to enhance the stewardship of time and resources. Without order there is chaos and confusion. God is not the author of confusion according to First Corinthians 14:33. Organization is necessary, institutionalization is not.

In the course of the discussion I make mention of *accountability*, which is a very important word in institutional Christianity. As used here, it refers to being answerable to and in full cooperation with the governing personnel and policies of an institution, a key factor in institutionalization. One who is not accountable to the institution is said to be *independent*. Just as the word's literal meaning indicates, someone who is 'without dependence' (upon a denomination) will tend to operate outside the accountability protocols of a denomination or other external controlling entity.

Two other words have definitions I want to clarify — e*mpowered* and *missional*. To be *empowered* is to be given permission, encouragement, opportunity and resources to undertake an endeavor. *Missional* is the opposite of institutional. To be missional is to make the accomplishing of the mission more important than the methods and systems created to accomplish it. Being missional implies being adaptable, flexible and responsive to new developments in order to maintain momentum toward the completion of the mission.

Acts 2:42-47 describes how the first Christ-followers met and fellowshipped together in each other's homes in Jerusalem and also continued with their temple-centered routine. As more and more people heard and responded to the gospel, three organizational necessities arose that started the followers of Jesus down the path toward the institutionalization of Christianity.

The first were the logistical challenges they encountered. As told in Acts 6, the Jerusalem church was faced with the sticky issue of how to equitably distribute food between the Aramaic and Greek-speaking widows. In the earlier days of the church, the Apostles had been in charge of food distribution. As the number of Christians grew into the thousands, it became apparent they needed help. The decision was made to select *"seven men from among* [the converts] *who* [were] *full of the Spirit and wisdom"* (Acts 6:3), and delegate the responsibility to them. In the Epistles, we see similar logistical issues that arose in the growing Christian community such as the collection and administration of benevolence funds (2 Corinthians 8-9), and protocols for observing the Lord's Supper (I Corinthians 11).

A second organizational necessity arose when the geographical expansion of Christianity made selecting new local leaders an issue. Decisions had to be made as to how they would go about identifying and installing overseers (I Timothy 3, Titus 1). Questions about determining the qualifications of such leaders and how they were to be installed had to be addressed.

The third challenge emerging Christianity faced was how to identify the 'truth'. There were many schools of thought and numerous writings by various authors circulating at the time. How were the Christians to maintain consistency with the teachings of Jesus and the Apostle's doctrine? Remember, it would be several hundred years before the Bible, as we know it today, would be compiled. One need only read Acts 15 or the Epistle to the Galatians to see what a struggle this was for the early church—and still is!

It is well documented historically how these three organizational imperatives came to occupy more and more of the Christian agenda. As the first generation Christians died and their converts and followers assumed leadership, more and more time and effort was put into administrating the money, selecting qualified leaders and riding herd on what was being taught. Inevitably, conflicts and disputes arose in the ranks. Complicating the matter further was the fact that, as a movement, the people who followed Jesus comprised the fastest growing and most widespread movement the world had ever seen. They were thought of as *hav*[*ing*] *turned the world upside down* (Acts 17:6).

Things progressed, often in the face of great persecution, until that fateful day when the Roman Emperor Constantine endorsed Christianity. Almost overnight the once persecuted Christian community transitioned into a role of status and political power. It became fashionable to convene great church councils to settle disputed issues… Was Jesus eternally divine? What benefit, if any, did Christ's death on the cross have for humanity? What is the composition and nature of the Godhead? Which writings in circulation are to be recognized as having canonical[6] authority? Who is the earthly head of the church? Emperor Constantine convened one of these councils, the Council at Nicaea, in 325 AD to settle a dispute about the divinity of Jesus and the concept of the Trinity.[7]

Of course, these were very important questions that could not be ignored. However, in their zeal to defend their points of view and remain aligned with the leaders and teachers they trusted, various factions emerged. Before long people were calling each other heretics, some groups of

"Christians" would have nothing to do with others, and some even went to war over property and doctrinal issues. At the Council of Nicaea, for example, one account of the proceedings relates that Saint Nicholas of Myra (the original Santa Claus) "show[ed] up at the council and [became] so angry with Arius that he [stood] up, walk[ed] across the chamber, and punch[ed] him".[8] Instead of being identified by their love one for another, Christians came to be more associated with their dogmas and creeds and accountability flow charts. It is interesting to note that the Council at Nicaea was presided over by the Emperor Constantine himself. Having militarily established peace throughout the empire, he didn't want these bickering Christians to spoil the peace. He "ordered" them to get along.[9] History records that after the council, under the emperor's watchful eye, produced the Nicene Creed, a number of its signatories promptly repudiated it as soon as they returned to their local settings.

All the while, and mostly behind the scenes, humble and sincere people of faith loved God and their neighbors. Led by the Spirit of truth within them, in simple and unpretentious ways, they encouraged one another, assisted the poor and sick, prayed and worshiped together. While the controversies raged in the halls of power and academia, the vast majority of Christ-followers were simply striving to live for Jesus the best they knew how. Christ continued to build his church as the "Holy Roman Empire" eventually disintegrated.

Later came what has been called the Age of Enlightenment and modernism. In a relatively condensed period of time there was an explosion of scientific discovery, literacy, knowledge, global travel and technology. On the heels of advancing knowledge came the quest for freedom, individual rights, and democracy. Coinciding with this came the Reformation and the birth of "free church" and congregational movements that were breaking away from the control of domineering State and Roman churches. Lutheran,

Presbyterian, Anglican, Wesleyan, Anabaptist and other movements took their place alongside the Roman Catholics on the Christian landscape, particularly in the western hemisphere. Elsewhere, various Orthodox and Coptic movements were entrenched. More recently, Holiness and Pentecostal movements have spawned numerous denominations, virtually all of them created as a new denomination as the result of controversy and discord.

It all has resulted in what I observed recently while driving through a small town in Middle America. On one city block near the center of town stood three imposing brick church buildings affiliated with three different denominations. Only a well-manicured strip of lawn separated their parking lots. They were elaborately constructed with religious adornment and with big marquees in front of each advertising their competing programs and schedules. I started thinking about how this same situation exists in cities large and small almost everywhere, especially in the United States. It seems that church buildings are in view at all times wherever one goes. And each one, as indicated by the sign out front, is affiliated with a different denomination or is proudly independent. (I tried to imagine the cumulative costs of just the maintenance and utilities for these facilities, especially when the vast majority of them stand mostly empty and unused during the week. Staggering!)

Why, I asked myself, does a little town of a few thousand people need all these church buildings? In this particular town, not only were there three buildings on the same block, there were three others that had been built more recently within two blocks of those! Why are Christians in communities small and large willing to separate themselves from their neighbors, friends, business associates, and even family members to 'worship' the same Lord on Sundays and study the same Bible on weeknights? Why are folks willing to give, often sacrificially, their hard earned money to keep open the doors of all these duplicated church buildings? After all the pragmatic explanations have been considered (e.g. outgrowing a facility or intentional church multiplication), one cannot ignore the fact that somewhere along the way, in the overwhelming majority of instances, there was a decision made by each distinctive group to separate itself from the others. A new group was started because of *dissatisfaction* with an existing one.

There are all kinds of reasons for this. Some want to follow a leader that others do not. Some want to emphasize a doctrine that others do not. Some want to worship in a style that others do not. Some are upset over a financial decision with which they did not agree. Some prefer a different color carpet in their church building. Bottom line, it is a my-way-or-the-highway mentality that has infected Christianity oftentimes. It is institutionalization run amok.

Search the founding documents and bylaws of any denomination or independent group and you will find the issue that precipitated the separation of that group from another. In the denomination of which I was a part, the primary issue was local congregational control of church properties. Other denominations emphasize modes of baptism, or how the clergy are designated, or how the sacraments are administered, or styles of attire, or day of worship, or path to membership; the list is endless. Even "independents" are often guilty of making their independence more important than Christ's mission. They have institutionalized, too.

What is one to make of all this? Since Christians believe Christ is the head of his Church, are we to assume that he was involved in the launching of all these factions and movements? To borrow a phrase from another current debate is there any evidence of *intelligent design* in the composition of Christianity today? Some might suggest that it wasn't necessarily how Jesus would have preferred it be done, but he has used it to his advantage nonetheless. If that is so, how has he used it to further the spread of the message of reconciliation? Are there any positive benefits we can point to in the rise and expansion of institutional Christianity and denominationalism?

On the positive side, one can point to incredible organized missionary endeavors that have been launched out of institutional Christianity. These endeavors have not only taken global the message of Jesus, they have also built medical clinics, hospitals, schools, and self-help programs. Denominationally sponsored agencies have played a big role.

Something can also be said in favor of the diversity that denominationalism has produced in Christianity. Whether one is of stern pious persuasion or celebrative, emotional disposition, there is a "brand" of Christianity that works for everyone. I see intelligent design in the evolution of Christianity that has enabled it to exist in every cultural setting. While the birth of most denominations came as a result of some disagreement initially, the diversification that resulted has furthered the extension of Christ's influence on earth.

Even in allowing his followers to struggle through the messy quest for doctrinal purity, one can see a certain genius in the Lord's plan. Each debate, each polarizing conflict over core beliefs has forced us, admittedly often against our will, to realize that there is always more to learn. It has had a refining and maturing effect upon the church. Imagine where Christianity would be today if no one ever called into question the teachings of the contemporaries of Jesus. If it continued to exist at all, Christianity would likely be a small Middle Eastern cult, still entrenched in Jerusalem, still practicing kosher laws, still prejudiced against Gentiles, still upholding slavery, and still treating women as second-class citizens.

What I'm suggesting is that the disputes, political games, control issues, intolerance and unresolved conflicts that have dogged Christianity from the beginning have not deterred the sovereign head of the church from getting us where we need to go. By design, Jesus handed off the propagation of the Gospel on earth to fallen, flawed, and spiritually/emotionally, immature human beings. Not because he was amused by the inept and, too often, harmful way we have gone about it; but rather, because he had a clear vision of where it would all lead. Jesus foresaw the day when *every knee should bow, in heaven and on earth and under the earth, and every tongue confess that Jesus Christ is Lord* (Philippians 2:10-11). Since the outcome of his mission to bring reconciliation to all was not in question, Jesus has been able to have patience with our process of growing up.

Reading the New Testament with an eye for the Lord's awareness that his followers would need to grow up, one will appreciate what he was saying in passages like Matthew 11:25: *At that time Jesus said, "I praise you, Father, Lord of heaven and earth, because you have hidden these things from the wise and learned, and revealed them to little children"*. The *little children* he was referring to here were his Apostles. And, as was mentioned earlier, Jesus knew his followers had a lot to learn, but at the time, they were not ready for him to tell them.

Both Paul and the writer of Hebrews understood that Christians have to go through a maturing process. To the Corinthians Paul wrote*: "Brothers, I could not address you as spiritual but as worldly—mere infants in Christ. I gave you milk, not solid food, for you were not yet ready for it. Indeed, you are still not ready"* (1 Corinthians 3:1-2). Earlier in the Epistle he hinted at God's plan for Christianity to go through a maturing process when he stated: *"Brothers, think of what you were when you were called. Not many of you were wise by human standards; not many were influential; not many* *were of noble birth. But God chose the foolish things of the world to shame the wise; God chose the weak things of the world to shame the strong. He chose the lowly things of this world and the despised things—and the things that are not— to nullify the things that are"* (1 Cor. 1:26-28). Drawing from his own experience and applying it to the spiritual journey we all must take, Paul wrote: *"When I was a child, I talked like a child, I thought like a child, I reasoned like a child. When I became a man, I put childish ways behind me. Now we see but a poor reflection as in a mirror; then we shall see face to face. Now I know in part; then I shall know fully, even as I am fully known"* (1 Corinthians 13:11-12).

The writer to the Hebrews admonished his readers to *"leave the elementary teachings about Christ and go on to maturity..."* (Hebrews 6:1). He envisioned a time when Christians would move beyond such elementary things as *"the foundation of repentance from acts that lead to death, and of faith in God, instruction about baptisms, the laying on of hands, the resurrection of the dead, and eternal judgment"* (Hebrews 6:1b-2). Church historians know that these are the very issues that have divided Christians and will continue to until we "grow up" enough to move on to a more mature spiritual focus.

As we proceed into the 21st century, we will see that denominationalism and institutional Christianity is losing its effectiveness and can no longer be thought of as promoting the best of the cause of Christ. I believe another phase of "maturity" is emerging before our very eyes.

I am not alone in my conclusion that denominations and their main enterprise, establishing works and programs that are loyal to and supportive of the denomination, are facing major change. Christian researcher and pollster, George Barna, asserts that traditional local churches will lose half their market share in the next ten years as growing numbers of people (20 million at the time his book was published) "leave the church to become the Church."[10] Whether or not those Barna identifies as "revolutionaries" will learn the lessons of the past and avoid the pitfalls of exclusion and institutionalization remains to be seen. I hope so. I pray so. Institutions that hope to remain vital in the 21st century will need to do whatever it takes to become empowering and missional. Few will.[11]

3

GOOD NEWS?

He said to them, "Go into all the world and preach the good news to all creation.
Mark 16:15

Yet when I preach the gospel, I cannot boast, for I am compelled to preach. Woe to me if I do not preach the gospel!
1 Corinthians 9:16

He was an intimidating figure, the pastor of the "largest Sunday school in America". The Sunday before I attended his Pastor's School, his church had thousands of people in Sunday school. I was 23 years old, the new pastor of my first church where maybe fifteen individuals had attended our Sunday school the week before. To say I was overwhelmed by it all is an understatement. I lost myself in the atmosphere generated by several thousand pastors and church leaders, many from the hard-line fundamentalist persuasion who, abuzz with expectation and eager to learn how to build their own mega Sunday schools, had packed out the biggest church sanctuary I had ever seen. It was 1974.

I should have known what I was in for when, as we were introducing ourselves to those seated nearby, a guy with a military haircut turned around to shake my hand, and after noticing my nametag identifying me as "Pastor Steve Rogers", sternly asked, "Do y'all have standards in your church?" Since neither his frown nor his drawled question were what I was accustomed to encountering in a "greeting time" in a church service, I thought perhaps I had misunderstood him and responded apologetically, "Excuse me, what did you say?" He condescendingly replied, "You're a pastor! Don't y'all have standards in your church? If you came to my church, my pastor would tell you to get a haircut." That was the first of several experiences that were to convince me, before the Pastor's School concluded that I must be one of those "compromising pussy footers" the host pastor would rail against throughout the week. To this guy, my 1974 hairstyle was obvious evidence of that. As the school continued, opportunities were given for those who wanted to get right with God by getting a haircut to "walk the aisle" and go to the room where they had a barber in-waiting. Although I didn't get up the courage to go forward, being the compromising pussy footer that I was, many others did. If the pastor said it once, he must have said it fifty times, "You don't like the way we do things around here? Well, how many did you have in Sunday school last Sunday?" What could I say? I had fifteen mostly old people; he had thousands that had come from as far as a hundred miles away on three hundred buses! If getting a haircut was part of the formula for success, who was I to question it?

Besides the buzz of hair clippers, there was a buzzword that was the theme of the week – SOULWINNING. It turned out that the reason to buy lots of buses, recruit volunteer bus captains, train them how to build a bus route, and grow a big Sunday school was to "win souls". A 'won' soul is a person who has heard the *Romans Road to Salvation*, or the *Five Steps to Heaven*, or the *Four Spiritual Laws*,[1] prayed a "Sinner's Prayer" (a sample of which appeared in the back of the booklet), starts attending Sunday school and other regular services, and gets rid of long hair and other "worldly" things like rock music. At the Pastor's School we learned how to recruit and train dutiful and dedicated bus captains and helpers who would go to their assigned neighborhoods and invite families, especially the kids, to get on the bus and come to Sunday school. "And guess what, kids," a captain might say, "This week we're going to have a clown giving away candy to all who come on our bus. Won't that be great?"

This particular church was the "Mecca" of bus ministry and fundamentalist soulwinning. Their Pastor's School featured various "heroic soulwinners" who were spotlighted like top sales people of the month at an Amway convention. This one had won several hundred souls last year. That one led more than 25 people to pray the Sinner's Prayer last week. This one led 5 people to Christ over the lunch hour!

The drumbeat continued: "You don't like the way we do it. How many did you have in Sunday school last Sunday?" By the end of the week I was wired and programmed to set my goals high and go for the big numbers. With the latest issue of *The Sword of the Lord* newspaper and a coupon in hand for that fundamentalist literary classic, *Bobbed Hair, Mini-skirts and Bossy Wives*, by John R. Rice, I returned home knowing what I had to do to get my church going and growing. It would be simple. Get a haircut, adopt uncompromising standards of holiness and modesty for all church members, start preaching from the *Scofield Reference Bible,* get busy being a soulwinner, and buy a bus as soon as possible. At first, it seemed like it was working. Within a week after returning home, I presented *The Five Steps to Heaven* to seventeen people who let me lead them in the Sinner's Prayer.

Notice I said these seventeen people "let me lead them in the Sinner's Prayer". What they did not do was join my church or any other one as far as I know. They did not become my friends. One family I had gotten to 'pray the prayer' sent word back to me that I was not to come around their house ever again. Apparently, I had developed some hard sell tactics that were effective for winning souls but not for winning friends. Come to think of it, my wife and parents weren't too excited about the new me either. My newly adopted harsh and legalistic manner alarmed them. They planned an intervention. I will forever be grateful for the day they sat me down and held up the 'mirror' to show me what I had become.

As the years have gone by, I've had experience with many other "schemes" of evangelism, outreach and church growth. Door-to-door surveys, telephone campaigns, crusades, revival meetings, "Bring a Friend" days, kid's carnivals, and a myriad of seeker events have all made their way onto my personal and church calendars. I'm sure most people who buy into these programs do so sincerely believing, as I did, that they are doing God's work and helping people connect with God. I have no doubt there are people who feel they have been brought closer to God because of the kind concern shown them by a sincerely motivated individual employing one of these strategies. Far be it from me to say otherwise; only God can measure all of that.

It has, however, caused me to probingly ask, is this really what Jesus had in mind when he told us to take the good news to all creation? Did Jesus ever imagine that we would take his words and make them proof texts for building huge religious organizations we call churches, institutions that expend vast amounts of time and resources to get people through their doors and into their seats, even if we have to shame or trick them to do so? I've had to honestly ask myself, did I want to be a soulwinner because of a deep and heartfelt burden for people separated from God? Or, more candidly, was it really because I wanted to build a church with big crowds so people would see me as successful? At best, my motives were mixed. And still it begs the question, is that what preaching the good news to all creation means?

"*For I am compelled to preach. Woe to me if I do not preach the gospel.*[2] As I read those remarks in their full context in First Corinthians 9, St. Paul seems to be saying that the satisfaction that comes from bringing good news[3] to people is highly motivating, so much so that he did not want to take payment for it. He never wanted his motive questioned or for money to get in the way of the relationship he was building with the Corinthians. Paul saw himself as an ambassador with a mission of reconciliation. He wrote to the Corinthians: "*So from now on we regard no one from a worldly point of view. Though we once regarded Christ in this way, we do so no longer. Therefore, if anyone is in Christ, he is a new creation; the old has gone, the new has come! All this is from God, who reconciled us to himself through Christ and gave us the ministry of reconciliation: that God was reconciling the world to himself in Christ, not counting men's sins against them. And he has committed to us the message of reconciliation. We are therefore Christ's ambassadors, as though God were making his appeal through us. We implore you on Christ's behalf: Be reconciled to God. God made him who had no sin to be sin for us, so that in him we might become the righteousness of God*" (2 Corinthians 5:16-21).

Helping people become aware that they have been reconciled to God through Christ is letting them in on some great news. God isn't counting our sins against us any longer! It is such great news that some have a hard time accepting it. It made Paul want to *implore* them *on Christ's behalf* to believe that nothing now stands in the way of a relationship with God. They (we) are reconciled – the whole world is!

It now makes me cringe when I think how I used to verbally corner people into admitting they were sinners separated from God and on their way to hell, coax them into repeating the prayer I told them to pray as if it is some magical formula, and then pressure them into giving up their Sundays and other spare time to come to my church. Good news? Reconciliation? Not!

In contrast, Jesus maintained that "[his] *yoke is easy and* [his] *burden is light*" (Matthew 11:30). In fact, when he got down to final instructions to his followers, he sent them forth with a rather simple assignment: *"Therefore go and make disciples of all nations, baptizing them in the name of the Father and of the Son and of the Holy Spirit, and teaching them to obey* **everything I have commanded you**. *And surely I am with you always, to the very end of the age"* (Matthew 28:19-20 emphasis mine). What exactly had Jesus **commanded** them? *"My command is this: Love each other as I have loved you"* (John 15:12).

How far removed from Jesus' central message is the soulwinner's witness I described above. When we attach to Jesus' gospel man made religious requirements such as having to maintain certain hair styles, avoid certain types of music, pray specifically worded prayers, attend regularly scheduled church services on certain days, adhere to specific doctrinal distinctions, give specified amounts of income, on and on the list goes, we are teaching something entirely different. And, it certainly does not come across as any kind of good news to people whose busy lives are already overwhelmed by daily obligations and performance evaluations.

This sort of regulating and shaming manipulation of people done in the name of Christ is precisely what Jesus wanted his followers to avoid. He cautioned: *"… do not do what [the teachers of the law and the Pharisees] do, for they do not practice what they preach. They tie up heavy loads and put them on men's shoulders"* (Matthew 23:3-4). Why? Jesus went on to explain: *"Everything they do is done for men to see..."* (23:5). As a former denominational insider who sat in a seat of authority on various boards and decision-making bodies, I know first hand, and have been guilty of, the posturing and power preservation that Jesus was describing. Words like prestige, hierarchy, power and control come into play whenever Christ's message morphs into a religious system and deviates from his one simple commandment to love one another.

    What if, by word and deed, the only message associated with Christians is, that we help others know that God loves them and so do we? What if, as Jesus indicated it would be, the only way anyone would ever know we were Christ's disciples is because we have *love one for another* (John 13:35)? What if we really did keep it as simple as just loving God and loving people? Personally, it is the central issue that sincere followers of Jesus Christ must face today. What are we doing that has needlessly encumbered and complicated the gospel? And, how are we to refocus the gospel back on its intended simplicity and make it truly wonderful good news for all?

4

THE B-I-B-L-E

All Scripture is inspired by God and is useful to teach us what is true and to make us realize what is wrong in our lives. It straightens us out and teaches us to do what is right. It is God's way of preparing us in every way, fully equipped for every good thing God wants us to do.
2 Timothy 3:16-17 NLT

You diligently study the Scriptures because you think that by them you possess eternal life. These are the Scriptures that testify about me, yet you refuse to come to me to have life.
John 5:39-40

"*The B-I-B-L-E, yes that's the book for me. I stand alone on the Word of God, the B-I-B-L-E.*" These are the words to the first song I recall learning as a child in Sunday school. We'd stand up in our Sunday best attire with neatly combed hair, hold our Bibles up in the air and sing it at the top of our lungs. We sang it weekly in Sunday school opening exercises and during our classes. It was an important ditty sung every day of vacation Bible schools and at elementary summer camps. Parents, teachers and pastors would smile proudly knowing they had successfully instilled in another generation the importance of the Bible.

Phrases like "the Word-o'-God", "the Bible says", or "according to the Scriptures" were as commonplace in our conversations as was talk of the weather. One would often hear, "If God said it that settles it, that's good enough for me." And we all knew whatever the speaker had just quoted from the Bible settled it—end of discussion—any further questioning or intellectual curiosity would be unnecessary. Disrespect for the authority of the person quoting the "Word-o'-God" was frowned upon. We learned, as good Christian boys and girls, to bring our doubts and ponderings of the mysteries of the divine into submission to the Bible expert *du jour*. And, even though it was stressed that the Bible was the *only* "inspired", "infallible" and "authoritative" guide to our faith and practice, only those who taught it the way we believed were to be trusted. By our standards, folks who read it differently were mishandling the Bible. The arrogance and intellectual inconsistency of this closed-minded way of thinking escaped our notice.

I vividly remember a discussion in a college class during which we were critical of a certain sect that referred to the Bible as being an important book in their tradition, "so long as it is correctly *translated*." This particular sect had, in effect, given writings other than the Bible more weight because they believed one couldn't properly interpret the Bible without looking through the lens of these other writings. This made it obvious to us that they were a cult. But the fact is we were guilty of exactly the same thing. We did not give the Bible the last word. We gave systematic theologies, doctrinal statements and those who interpreted the scriptures consistent with our tradition the last word. If anyone arrived at conclusions other than our own regarding what the Bible was saying, we suspected some extra-biblical authority was misleading them. We, on the other hand, were unquestioningly submitted to the authority of the "Word-o'-God" – as long as it was correctly *interpreted.*

From the earliest days of my encounter with the love of Christ in the Jesus Movement of the early 1970's, I had a deep desire to study the Bible. At the age of nineteen I began a love affair with the Scriptures. I have devoted my entire adult life to reading, studying, meditating upon, preaching, teaching, discussing, and writing about the Bible. It is my primary written source of spiritual wisdom. It amazes me that after all these years, having read it so many times, it continues to instruct me with freshness and new insight. Which is to say, I have revised my understanding of what it teaches over and over? On some things I have actually come to understand the Bible to say the *opposite* of what I once thought it said! I suppose that is what Apostle Paul was indicating when he said he had "*put away childish things*" (I Corinthians 13:11).

I can accept that God *breathed* upon those who wrote the content of the Bible and guided its compilation and preservation through history. There is a very, very short list of literary works that have been passed from one generation to the next over the course of thousands of years. Among them, only the Bible, remains perennially at the top of the best seller lists. Most other books are forgotten within a year or less of publication. The Bible has stood the test of time. However, believing in the inspiration of Scripture is not the same thing as believing that my ability to quote from the Bible gives me authority to tell other people how to live and what to believe, especially when they haven't asked for my input. To expect that people who do not share my respect for the Bible will automatically acquiesce to something I quote from it as the last word is unreasonable. But, to the dismay of many, that is exactly what Bible-loyal Christians try to do all the time. It is this tendency that has given rise to pejoratives such as "Bible thumper" or "fundamentalist".

I think of it this way. If I came into the home a person who didn't speak English, started bossing him around in English, and then showed impatience with his slowness to comply with my demands of how he should run his home, he'd be justified in wanting me to shut up and get out of his house as quickly as possible. That is, in effect, what many Bible authoritarians do. They have diligently studied the Scriptures, developed a tribal language of 'Bible-speak' that only people from their 'tribe' can understand, and believe everybody else should accept their word on a variety of subjects. Some go to considerable effort and expense to recruit others into their way of thinking.

Of course, some will argue that our culture was once Bible-based and has strayed from its heritage, contending that, if folks don't understand or appreciate our biblical heritage, it's not due to any fault of the Bible believers. They insist it is those who have abandoned the Bible who are speaking the wrong language and are the rude and inconsiderate ones. Back and forth the argument has gone, until we have the tension that exists today. The Bible authoritarians are stiffening in their biblical dogmatism and the others are growing increasingly intolerant of the Bible people. It truly is a culture war.

Lately, I'm reconsidering where I stand on the matter. It's not that I want to join the ranks of those who have a low regard for the Bible. I still love the Scriptures and look to them for godly wisdom and guidance. It's just that I've grown increasingly uncomfortable with the tendency I see in some Bible authoritarians to ignore what the Bible says. For example, in Matthew 5:39-44, Jesus is quoted as saying, *"But I tell you, do not resist an evil person. If someone strikes you on the right cheek, turn to him the other also. And if someone wants to sue you and take your tunic, let him have your cloak as well. If someone forces you to go one mile, go with him two miles. Give to the one who asks you, and do not turn away from the one who wants to borrow from you. "You have heard that it was said, 'Love your neighbor and hate your enemy.' But I tell you: Love your enemies and pray for those who persecute you."* Unfortunately, it has been my experience that the more biblically authoritarian (dogmatic) one's views, the more resistant and intolerant one tends to be toward others of differing views. The result ends up being the very opposite of what Jesus was teaching in the above passage. How else can it be explained that Bible-quoting 'Christians' are some of the most xenophobic, pro-war people on the planet today?

The Apostle Paul taught the Corinthians a common sense principle of being sensitive to people who come from a different background. Addressing how they were using the gift of tongues in public gatherings he wrote, *"So if the whole church comes together and everyone speaks in tongues, and some who do not understand or some unbelievers come in, will they not say that you are out of your mind?"* (1 Corinthians 14:23). He then instructed that, in order to avoid this kind of confusion and miscommunication, care should be taken to interpret what is being spoken so everyone in the room can respond. To do otherwise is arrogant, rude, and does more harm than good. It is a matter of basic hospitality and courtesy as anyone who has been left out while a foreign language was being spoken can attest. I've personally experienced far too many Bible authoritarians who act as if such a call for good manners doesn't apply to them. In disrespecting others who do not read and interpret the Bible as they do, these folks disrespect the very Bible they claim to defend. Isn't this the same hypocrisy that Jesus confronted so forcefully in his time?

Earlier, I suggested that many Bible-loyal people are of the opinion that it is not their fault the culture has moved away from holding the Bible in high regard. However, I've come to think we should accept some of the blame for the low regard many have of the Bible in our society. If large segments of the population view Bible-toting Christians as narrow minded, mean-spirited, intolerant hypocrites, they may have good reason. While I would like to believe that most Bible-loyal people are good hearted, sincerely motivated individuals who don't wish to create an offense or erect barriers that keep people from valuing the Scriptures, it must be remembered that one of the first rules of communication is that the listener ultimately determines the message communicated. I may say something to you with the kindest of intentions, but if you hear it as aggressive and threatening, then that's what has been communicated. If clear communication is the goal, the speaker must take special care that her listener is hearing what she means to say. Who can deny that far too many of us have stood upon the authority of our interpretation of the Bible and railed against the culture in threatening tones? Bible authoritarians have weighed in on this or that social or political issue (I choose not to be specific in this context) as if they are the voices of God, and have verbally cornered and put on the defensive all who would question their declaration of "truth". The rejection and invalidation of others is palpable sometimes. No wonder comments are made such as one spoken by a TV comedian, who, when referring to Bible authoritarians said, "These people scare me!" What a contrast that is when compared to how the populace of his day responded to Jesus. Mark 12:37 says, *"The large crowd listened to him with delight."*

However, while employing a more polite and considerate approach in presenting a Bible-based perspective will help resolve some of this tension and is a good place to start, it won't solve the bigger problem underlying the culture war.

As long as one group thinks that what they believe is the standard by which everyone is to be judged and accepted or rejected by God, people are going to be at odds. As long as some believe it is their mandate from God to convert others to their beliefs, we're going to have culture wars.

Jesus stated that *he* is *"the way, the truth and the life"* (John 14:6). As a Christian, I take that to mean Jesus is the embodiment and visible example of the truth and the life to which it leads. As a believer in Jesus, I expect that anyone discovering truth will discover Jesus eventually. Jesus promised that after he departed, there would come *"another Counselor to be with you forever—the Spirit of truth"* (John 14:16-17) ... who would *"guide you into all truth... by taking what is mine and making it known to you"* (John 16:13-14). This is no small matter. Jesus taught that it would be the operation of the Spirit of truth in the world that would lead the world into the truth (John 16:8-11). If this is true, I don't need to feel threatened if some folks disagree with me at the moment. I can be encouraged in the knowledge that while the Spirit of truth continues to work in me to guide me toward realizing what is true; he's working in everyone else as well. I'm far better off if I remain focused on following the Spirit's lead in addressing my own issues, rather than presuming it's my mission to straighten out everyone else's thinking.

Clearly, Jesus knew and quoted the Scriptures of his time, yet there is little indication that he considered a background in these Scriptures as a *prerequisite* to encountering God. In fact, his was a contrarian approach to the traditional understanding of Scripture, as taught by the main religious parties of his day, and it got him into trouble. Take note of how many times Jesus made this statement in the Sermon on the Mount, *"You have heard that it was said... but I tell you..."* (Matthew 5-7). The Bible authoritarians of his day understood him to be setting his teaching against their deeply held understanding of the Scriptures. In answer to questions they would disingenuously throw at him, he would often challenge them to quote what exactly the Scriptures said in order to point out how far from the truth they were in their interpretations. The recounting of the story of the Good Samaritan is a good example (Luke 10:25-37). Jesus could not have been more controversial than he was in telling the parable of the Good Samaritan. By contrasting the mercifulness of the Samaritan with the indifference of the priest and the Levite, who were normally regarded to be models of uprightness, Jesus directly challenged both their understanding of Scriptures and standards of piety.

I know of no place in the Bible where Jesus told those who would follow him that a Bible certification course would be required for qualified disciples. Although he modeled having knowledge of the Scriptures and must have felt they were important, he stressed that it was the Holy Spirit's role to guide us into the truth—with or without the Bible. Jesus fully understood that one can know the truth and not know the Bible, and one can know the Bible and not know the truth.[1]

That is why I have come to regard authoritarian applications of the Bible as troublesome, if not even dangerous. When Christians make statements such as, "We believe the Bible is the inspired Word of God and the only infallible guide and rule of our faith and practice" (a common evangelical doctrinal statement), are we not saying that without the Bible one cannot know God, or how to believe, or how to live? Even though Jesus emphasized it would be the Spirit who would guide us into truth, this type of statement asserts that it is the Bible and only the Bible that does so. And, since they believe that knowing the Bible is so necessary to godly living, the folks who adhere to this rigid doctrinal stance tend to make it their primary objective to convert everyone to their study methods and *interpretation* of the Bible. Since followers of Jesus existed for centuries without the Bible as it exists today, it obviously can't be the *only* infallible guide to faith and practice. Illiteracy is not an impediment to love or the Spirit of God.

I believe people who never learned to read but whose spiritual life was nurtured in the relational context of story telling and "one-anothering" will populate heaven—Spirit-led people who had no exposure to the studying, lectures and note-taking that so characterize how modern Western Christians "do" Christianity. "According to the 2004 Lausanne paper *Making Disciples of Oral Learners,* nearly 90 percent of the world's Christian workers serve among auditory learners and often use inappropriate, literacy-based communication styles."[2] The message that is being communicated from our modern epistemology is that, unless you have biblical literacy you are spiritually ignorant; and, because we have it, we know more than you. If you want to be one of us you must study and learn the Bible as we teach it.

I'll say it again—I love the Bible. I want everyone who can to read it, study it, meditate upon it and follow its teachings. But, I'd like to see an attitude displayed by all Bible-lovers that is reflective of the fact that it is a book comprised of wisdom literature, poetry, prophecies, symbolism, allegory, metaphor, editorial, mystery, apocalyptic styling, and parable, as well as material specific to individuals, ancient culture and events. That means it has to be interpreted, and our interpretations are subjective. Bible students of the highest academic qualifications do not agree on many of its meanings. Even if one accepts that the Bible is inspired of God, as I do, we have to admit that our *interpretations* probably aren't inspired and certainly not infallible. Further, anyone who has matured, evolved, or altered in any way his or her understanding of what the Bible is saying must readily admit that there is still so much one can learn. We haven't been led into all the truth yet. We continue to *"know in part,"* as Paul put it in I Corinthians 13:9.

My suggestion to all who want to bring a biblical worldview to the forefront is to be gentle. Offer your biblical opinions in the context of relationships where mutual respect and trust have been cultivated. Those who wish to be heard must first be listeners. Consider the possibility that others may have something important to say about life and spirituality that you need to learn as well. For me, it places the emphasis on the "how I live" being more important than the "what I know". And since what I know may change as the Spirit guides me into more truth, I ought to be very humble and not authoritarian about what I perceive from the Scriptures at any given time. Discipleship should be viewed as a Holy Spirit-guided journey toward intimacy with God and toward love for one's neighbors, rather than as the cognitive mastering of Bible information for the purpose of being able to win the argument.

5

WHAT'S WRONG WITH THIS PICTURE?

*"For my thoughts are not your thoughts,
neither are your ways my ways,"
declares the* LORD.
*"As the heavens are higher than the earth,
so are my ways higher than your ways
and my thoughts than your thoughts."*
Isaiah 55:8-9

One thought has been nagging me since my days in Bible college when I was first exposed to the debate between the Augustinian (Calvinistic) and Arminian ways of interpreting the Bible. I was raised in the Arminian tradition that emphasizes the role our behavioral choices have in bringing us into and maintaining right standing with God. We were clearly taught that if we died before confessing and repenting of our bad conduct we would be immediately separated from God and sent to eternally roast in hell. The reason? Holy God could not allow any sin or its carriers, we sinners, into his heaven. (The fact that Satan seemed to show up in heaven from time to time as the Book of Job indicates seemed to have escaped our teaching!) Other than an occasional jab from the pulpit at those misguided folks who believed in something referred to as "once saved always saved", I had no exposure to any other way of understanding the Bible, and no reason to question the Arminian tradition.

Here I was in Bible college and, although the emphasis was upon disproving it, I now was learning there were lots of other Christians who used the Bible to teach an entirely different perspective – Calvinism. The Calvinists seemed to be saying that personal choice had little if anything to do with one's standing with God. Rather, it was God's choices that were the all-important factor. We couldn't 'choose God' unless he first chose us. If he first chose us we were destined to choose him. If you didn't choose him it was because you weren't first chosen. The fix was in so to speak. I also discovered that some people really liked to argue about this stuff.

One day it dawned on me why the two sides were (and are) so passionate about defending their positions. It occurred to me that both groups were desperately trying to cling to their "own salvation" by defending the formula they think got them "saved". Arminians do not want to give up their equity in personal holiness and hard work to please God, so any suggestion that once saved a person could not become unsaved is like saying once saved a person can live any way he wants—and that just couldn't be right as they see it. The Calvinists, on the other hand, do not want to give up their elected status by linking it with "feeble" good works. They contend they didn't earn their salvation by their good works, so why should it be possible to lose salvation by any absence of good works? The Arminians are counting on *their decision* to accept Christ and subsequent ongoing obedience to get them into heaven; Calvinists are counting on their *predestined election* to get them in. Both arguments left me with more questions than answers. Trying to reconcile these two points of view, for a time I opted to believe that I had taken the Arminian path of making a "free will" decision for Christ initially, and that Calvinism, because my place in heaven was secure from there on in, had relieved the pressure to constantly get "resaved". I long ago gave up arguing about it, concluding that both were insufficient points of view and debating them was a waste of time.

As I have observed how divided Christians become over such matters, I have developed a growing distaste for and mistrust of dogmatic doctrinal positions. Rather than take an inflexible stand based upon the opinions of dead theologians, I've found myself gravitating toward a deeper respect for the mystery of God. As God said in Isaiah 55:8-9, *"For my thoughts are not your thoughts, neither are your ways my ways," declares the* Lord. *"As the heavens are higher than the earth, so are my ways higher than your ways and my thoughts than your thoughts."* That being true, it seems rather silly (and presumptuous) of us to think our doctrinal schemes have it all figured out.

I am struck by how unorthodox Jesus came across to the orthodoxy of his day. He confronted the religious scholars and Pharisees (the conservative defenders of the faith) over the fact that when reading the Scriptures they had missed the point. The Scriptures spoke of him, Jesus said, but they couldn't see it. Their Bible study had also led them to the erroneous conclusion that no prophet could come from Galilee, Jesus' home town. In John 9, Jesus went so far as to claim they were clueless about God, the Father, because if they had truly known God they would have recognized him, Jesus of Nazareth, as God's Son. It makes me wonder if the "orthodoxy" has ever gotten it right. I think the concept of orthodoxy as defined by the majority opinion of trusted "authorities" is very vulnerable to missing the point.

One doesn't have to search very far in the historical record to uncover multiple paradigm shifts that have resulted in the evolution of orthodoxy. Truth defenders have thumped their Bibles in defense of now largely discarded doctrines such as believing the earth is flat, claiming the inferiority of certain races, defending anti-Semitism in many despicable forms, justifying slavery, insisting in male ownership and dominance of women, and more. All of these doctrines were, at various times in church history, the deeply held beliefs of the mainstream Christian orthodoxy. Yet, now that such Bible "truths" have been discredited and have given way to what one supposes to be more enlightened biblical understanding, we find alternative views that were once considered to be heresy (and for which people who held them were tortured and killed) are in the mainstream of Christian thinking. Orthodoxy is a fickle business.

The more I think about it the more absurd it seems that Christians divide over issues like these. How inappropriate it is for any group to think they have God's ways all figured out and to behave like they are authorized to straighten out everybody else's thinking. We're no better than the Bible scholars of Jesus' day who "diligently studied the Scriptures" but missed the truth by a mile. We proof text and string together arguments based upon man-made interpretive schemes and human reason and, then, come up with conclusions that are possibly as erroneous as the one drawn by those who were scripturally certain Jesus couldn't be a prophet because he came from Galilee (John 7:52).

Philosopher Thomas Talbott has pointed out the weakness of both Calvinism and Arminianism by offering a set of three inconsistent propositions.[1] Talbott's propositions are:

1. God's redemptive love extends to all human sinners equally in the sense that he sincerely wills or desires the redemption of each one of them.
2. Because no one can finally defeat God's redemptive love or resist it forever, God will triumph in the

end and successfully accomplish the redemption of everyone whose redemption he sincerely wills or desires.
3. Some human sinners will never be redeemed but will instead be separated from God forever.

Talbott points out that Calvinists take a position that combines propositions 2 and 3. Arminians, on the other hand, gravitate toward the combination of 1 and 3. Obviously, one cannot logically affirm all three to be true at the same time. What is particularly interesting to me is how both the Calvinists and Arminians hold to proposition 3 in their doctrinal construct. Both camps hold to a view that *excludes* lots of people.

I'm more than a little suspicious as to why both camps find it necessary to exclude so many from God's redemptive grace. Whether salvation is dependant upon God's choice or human choice, as the Calvinists and Arminians would have it, most people who have ever lived come out on the wrong side of the choice. What lies behind this need to exclude? Why must we always have an *included/excluded* dichotomy? The *a priori* assumption of the traditional Calvinistic and Arminian positions is that a sizeable percentage of the human race goes to eternal damnation, and that it is good and proper (ultimately God's will) that it is so. That troubles me deeply. It has weighed on me for years. Both sides of the debate defend their perspectives vigorously using the Bible, and often quote the exact same proof texts with entirely different excluding interpretations. I join Talbott and others in proposing: Since nobody who is thinking rationally would ever *prefer* eternal damnation as their ultimate end, and since God is on record saying he is not willing that any *perish* (2 Peter 3:9), shouldn't the *a priori* assumption be that no one will end up excluded from God's grace and eternally damned? It seems to me our starting point should be that somehow everyone is encompassed in God's redemption through Jesus Christ—no one is excluded.

Staunch defenders of these exclusionary mindsets will quickly appeal to their biblical proof texts as the reason, but I'm convinced there are other reasons. I suspect if we could clear away all the hermeneutical *Twister* games the dogmatic debaters like to play in arriving at their exclusionary conclusions, we would discover the same mishandling of the Scriptures that characterized so many of the Bible scholars of Jesus' day. And, if that is true, what we might realize is that the need to exclude others who haven't conformed to a particular doctrinal perspective is not really based on faithfulness to God's Word as much as it is on a basic human psychological need – the need to protect and defend oneself and his or her turf at the expense of another. It is a personal security issue of needing to know who is a part of my tribe and who is an outsider.

As we go back to Genesis and read the account of the temptation and fall of Adam and Eve, we see the starting point of this defensiveness and self-protection – the exclusionary *me vs. you* (us vs. them) approach to life. First, Adam blamed Eve for his sin in order to justify himself. Their son, Cain, subsequently killed his brother, Abel, to preserve his own dignity. Later, people groups and kingdoms formed, leading to boundary disputes, political conflicts, competing tribal religions, power struggles, and wars.[2] In the New Testament, we learn that the biggest controversy among the early Christ followers centered on Jew and Gentile cultural and religious separation. The 'law vs. grace' issue that is so prevalent in the writings of St. Paul was all about the need of some to identify who would be considered 'in' and who would not qualify for inclusion.

I suspect that many of the elaborately explained and defended dogmas of some groups today are little more than a sophisticated form of this same sort of *tribalism* – a complex system of identifiers around which people form a community wherein they find protection, value and distinction from others. Thus, in circles where "denomination-speak" is spoken, you will hear phrases like "our doctrinal distinctives". In other words, we provide this list of our particular doctrines so that everyone else will understand why we think our group (tribe) is to be distinguished from (more correct than) the others.[3]

Whether one adheres to Calvinism, Arminianism or whatever other *'ism'*, I've come to believe it is generally more about staking out a comfort zone of personal identity than it is the defense God's truth. Rather than try to categorize folks and decide which of them are saved and which of them are not saved, I've come to realize that everyone is a member-in-process of God's redeemed family. That changes my mission from feeling compelled to make converts of others to my "orthodoxy" so they can be included in my tribe, to loving them as fellow pilgrims on the journey into God's mercy and joy. We are all in God's tribe!

6

BLACK CAT

"Do not repay anyone evil for evil. Be careful to do what is right in the eyes of everybody. If it is possible, as far as it depends on you, live at peace with everyone. Do not take revenge, my friends, but leave room for God's wrath, for it is written: it is mine to avenge; I will repay," says the Lord. On the contrary: "If your enemy is hungry, feed him; if he is thirsty, give him something to drink. In doing this, you will heap burning coals on his head. Do not be overcome by evil, but overcome evil with good."
Romans 12:17-21

When I was in junior high, I lived across the street from an outdoor ice-skating rink. One of our favorite pastimes in the cold of winter was to lace up our skates and join with the many who would head over after supper to skate under the lights. The loud speakers mounted on the light poles played Top 40 songs. The charcoal heater in the shelter would take the numbness out of our toes so we could get back out on the ice to flirt with the rosy-cheeked girls in their white figure skates and matching mittens and scarves. One end of the ice was always taken over by those who were playing the game we called "Black Cat."

Black Cat on ice skates was fast-paced, competitive and could be dangerous. We'd start the game by selecting someone who would be the Black Cat. His part in the game would be to skate to the middle of the rink and face the rest of us who would line up along the edge of the ice – us against him. He would call out "Black Cat!" and that would be the signal for us to skate as fast as we could toward the other side of the ice. The Black Cat would try to tag (touch) as many of us as possible before we could get past him. Any of us who were tagged before we could skate to the safe zone on the other side, would then be "adopted" into the Black Cat's team to try to tag the remaining others when "Black Cat" was again shouted. Again, it was "us" against "them". It usually took several passes before all had been tagged. Some of the better skaters who could go fast and stop on a dime could evade capture for quite awhile, but eventually the numbers against them were too great and they could not escape. The game ended when all were on the same team. "We" had become "them". I like to think of God engaging us in a game of Black Cat.

Since the beginning, the fallen human race ("us") has tried to get away from Father, Son and Holy Spirit, the triune God ("them", figuratively speaking).[1] In response, God set about to "touch" all who had aligned against him and were running from him. The Lord is constantly pursuing us to touch us with his grace and love and welcome us onto his "team".

How and why? The answer is found in the life, death and resurrection of Jesus Christ. God became a human being in the person of Jesus of Nazareth. He subjected himself to the full range of human experience—infancy, puberty, training, labor, pleasure, grief, pain, hunger, fatigue, love, rejection, temptation, feeling cut off from God, and a hideous death. John wrote that God reached toward us in loving embrace when, *"The Word became flesh and lived for a while among us"* (John 1:14). According to 2 Corinthians 5:21, Christ was even *"made to be sin for us."* As incredible as the embrace of living among us for awhile may seem, that the Son of God incarnate also was *"made to be sin for us"*, putting himself in our skates, takes the discussion to a whole different level.[2]

The explanation the Bible provides for why God lived for a while among us is LOVE. *"Because of his great love..."* (Ephesians 2:4), *"God demonstrates his own love for us..."* (Romans 5:8), *"For God so loved the world..."* (John 3:16), and other passages, all speak to the point that God was motivated by love to interface with sin-broken humanity. As a consequence of God's expressed love, we are *"accepted in the beloved"* (Christ).[3] *"Because of his great love for us, God, who is rich in mercy, made us alive **with Christ** even when we were dead in transgressions—it is by grace you have been saved. And God raised us up **with Christ** and seated us with him in the heavenly realms in Christ Jesus* (Ephesians 2:3-6 emphases added). No longer, as far as God is concerned, is it a situation of 'us against them'. Now, we are said to be "in Christ". Everything that had separated us from God has been removed. Now there is no dividing wall between them (the Trinity) and us. God is in us. We are in God. Reconciled. Writing to the Galatians, Paul went so far as to say that when Jesus was crucified, we were, in effect, crucified with him (Galatians 2:20). When Jesus was resurrected, so were we. Something happened that changed the status of sin-damaged humans from being excluded from God to being included in God. Once we were on the outside, now we're on the inside. Once we were strangers and aliens, now we are children and heirs. Once we were lost, now we are found. Once we were enemies of God, now we are friends.[4]

God initiated and did some very counter-intuitive things to pull this off. For example, Psalm 103:10 tells us, *"...he does not treat us as our sins deserve."* Similarly, Paul wrote, *"God was reconciling the world to himself in Christ, not counting men's sins against them"* (2 Corinthians 5:19).

Our human sense of justice tells us sin must be punished in a reciprocal manner appropriate to the offense. To not treat us "as our sins deserve", cuts across the grain of everything we'd expect from a just God. We are told that Jesus *"made himself nothing taking the very nature of a servant"* (Phil. 2:7). God voluntarily turning himself into a servant certainly is not what anyone would expect of the sovereign Creator. Further, the Bible tells us that Jesus *"learned obedience from what he suffered"* (He. 5:8). The Synoptic Gospels portray Jesus in an agonizing struggle to bring his will into alignment with the will of *Abba*[5] at Gethsemane (e.g. Mark 14:36). Jesus was able to connect his suffering with God's unfolding purpose for his life in a manner that taught him to walk in consistent obedience. Suffice it to say that God put forth extraordinary *unilateral* effort in Christ's coming and dwelling among us. I emphasize unilateral because, *"God demonstrates his own love for us in this: **While we were still sinners**, Christ died for us"* (Romans 5:8 emphasis added).

Meanwhile, as Christ's redemption works its way into creation and the consciousness of humankind (*"Thy kingdom come, thy will be done on earth as it is in heaven"*),[6] we continue to encounter circumstances that violate our sense of justice and fairness. Anyone with a sibling can attest to repeated incidents of seeming unfairness. Everyone encounters a bully sooner or later. Most of us have stories to tell of defrauding by others. We've all been vandalized in some way. Far too many know outright abuse at the hand of another. People insult us, gossip and tell lies about us. People judge us by the color of our skin, the neighborhoods we live in, the clothes we wear, the schools we attend, and the shape of our bodies. The holocausts, ethnic or religious cleansings, and acts of terrorism that have left ugly scars upon human history attest to the extremity of the meanness with which we can deal with each other. Cycles of violence are passed from one generation to the next. In the name of saving face and vengefully righting a wrong, the most hateful and brutal acts are committed. Add into the mix the violent crimes conceived in the sin-darkened minds of sick and psychologically warped individuals who prey upon the innocent, and the picture gets even bleaker. We are all jaded because we've been wronged by someone inclining us toward that state of being described in Romans 3:13-17: "[Our] *throats are open graves;* [our] *tongues practice deceit.' 'The poison of vipers is on* [our] *lips.'* '[Our] *mouths are full of cursing and bitterness.'* '[Our] *feet are swift to shed blood; ruin and misery mark* [our] *ways, and the way of peace* [we] *do not know.'"*

Even when we are able to restrain and internalize our anger over being unjustly treated and resist responding with violence, we all know the thoughts of ill will toward others that go through our minds as we fantasize about how we would like to see them get what they deserve. Peace is usually the farthest thing from what we are thinking. So, while it is true that we have been reconciled to God, we have a long way to go before we're reconciled to each other.

In order to redeem this situation, God has implemented a *long-range* strategy whereby the good news of his reconciling grace through Christ will touch each of us. Being so "tagged" by his grace, we are empowered by the Holy Spirit to follow Jesus' example when dealing with our earthly enemies, in order that reconciliation will touch them, too. In the end we all will be on God's team.

This is a difficult idea for many to grasp. It is predicated upon someone deciding to *'turn the other cheek.'* Jesus gave us the example to follow.

God was mindful of our very human inclination toward vengeance and in an effort to curtail the rampant violence that was the norm he instructed Moses: *"Show no pity: life for life, eye for eye, tooth for tooth, hand for hand, foot for foot,"* (Deuteronomy 19:21). The Law of Moses stipulated wrongdoers were only to be proportionally punished. However, the biblical record later fills in the detail that this was a temporary accommodation on God's part. Writing to the Galatians, Paul explained that the Old Covenant law was like a tutor – a temporary guardian/trustee who was put in charge of the youngsters until such time as they were mature enough to assume full responsibility in the family affairs (Galatians 4:1-3). As Paul went about championing the New Covenant in Christ, his message was that the day had now arrived when the Old Covenant tutoring was no longer necessary. Vengeance in human affairs was now to be rejected and allowed to go the way of all that was abolished when Christ's death *abolished* the law (Ephesians 2:15).[7]

In addition to providing the social and religious order for the fledgling nation of the children of Israel, the Law of Moses revealed to the human family a very important reality we needed to learn about ourselves. Paul summed it up, *"I would not have known what sin was except through the law"* (Romans 7:7). But, he also pointed out that there was no inherent power in the Old Covenant law to change a heart or transform a society (Romans 8:3; Galatians 2:15-16, 3:11). I think of it as God saying to Old Covenant generations, "I know that mistreatment at the hand of others brings pain and anger. For now, you may react harshly to wrongdoing. Go ahead and get even with those who misbehave and offend you unjustly. After you've gone that route for a while, you are going to discover that getting even with the other guy doesn't fix the problem. And, you're also going to realize, in one way or another, that you do the same things that those who wronged you have done. You're really no better than they are when you get right down to it, but I will be taking care of that dilemma in due time by coming to live among you and laying down my life to free you from it."

Sure enough, folks were figuring this out by the time of Christ. They understood that trying to live up to the law with its 'shalls and shall nots' of dealing with God and our fellow humans, was, as Peter put it, *"a yoke that neither we nor our fathers have been able to bear"* (Acts 15:10). No matter how they tried to reinforce living according to the law with myriad formulas and rules for everything, they could not. Tevya, the lead character in the Broadway production and movie, *Fiddler on the Roof,* wryly observes that the *eye for an eye and a tooth for a tooth* approach only results in everyone becoming "blind and toothless," a phrase borrowed from Gandhi. Everyone is guilty of something—a point St. Paul developed at length in Romans 2 and 3. Vengeful responses to being wronged are understandable, but they have never worked to heal pain and resolve the problem.

The life and message of Jesus is the alternative. If the Jesus story tells us anything, it tells us that the path to reconciliation requires someone to go to the effort of unilaterally reaching out to the other side. In Jesus, we see the supreme example of it. As noted, Jesus entered into human suffering and experienced the challenges that obedience to God present to human beings. He was able to navigate through the temptation survival course without sin (Hebrews 4:15), but the experience gave him a clear understanding of why we feebler souls are unable to do so on our own. And because of that, the very next verse invites us to *"approach the throne of grace with confidence, so that we may receive mercy and find grace to help us in our time of need"* (Hebrews 4:16).

When God stepped into our ice skates, playing on both sides of the Black Cat game, he encountered every enticement to sin and evil that we do. The instructional suffering[8] and incessant temptation he encountered during his earthly sojourn left Jesus very aware of what we go through and feeling quite sympathetic to the weaknesses that so limit how we respond to it. Consequently, we can be free of all insecurity and fear as we approach God. He sits on a *throne of grace* and renews to us daily his compassionate *mercy* (Lamentations 3:22-23), precisely because he knows how we feel and what we're going through. Knowing what he knows and experiencing what he experienced of our weaknesses, God has determined that he will not deal with us as our sins deserve. To do so would be an injustice by God's standards.

7

DISCIPLINE FOR THE "HELL" OF IT

"Our fathers disciplined us for a little while as they thought best; but God disciplines us for our good..."
Hebrews 12:10

Years ago, our adolescent son accidentally broke a window in our house with a golf ball. It was a mistake resulting from immature decision making on his part. His mother and I understood that his "transgression" was a product of immaturity and 'weakness'. In keeping with the demeanor of loving parents, we did not demand, out of a wrathful need for the satisfaction of our parental sense of justice, that he be punished. *Because* we sympathized with his 'weakness', we had neither the need nor the desire to demand vengeance. We did, however, ask him to help us pay for the window from his allowance as a way of reinforcing in him the wisdom of not standing in the front yard and hitting golf balls toward the house. We had freedom to choose an instructive response that prepared him to have better judgment in the future because we fully expected Erik would learn from his mistake and be less inclined to repeat it.

Webster's tells us *"discipline"* is *"training that corrects, molds, or perfects the mental faculties or moral character."* Our training seemed "painful" and unpleasant to our son, but it was temporary and ultimately was for his benefit and the good of our relationship. This is the very point made in Hebrews 12:7-11: *"Endure hardship as discipline; God is treating you as sons. For what son is not disciplined by his father? If you are not disciplined (and everyone undergoes discipline), then you are illegitimate children and not true sons. Moreover, we have all had human fathers who disciplined us and we respected them for it. How much more should we submit to the Father of our spirits and live! Our fathers disciplined us for a little while as they thought best; but God disciplines us for our good, that we may share in his holiness. No discipline seems pleasant at the time, but painful. Later on, however, it produces a harvest of righteousness and peace for those who have been trained by it."* No one escapes for very long the reality that life has its hardships, and behavior has its consequences. It can be comforting to realize that at work in it all, though not necessarily the cause is a loving Heavenly Father who disciplines us for our good with the ultimate objective of bringing us into *righteousness and peace.*

Too many of us have failed to appreciate the fact that throughout the Old and New Testaments are many descriptions of God as good and merciful. Moses, for example, revealed his understanding of the nature of God when he prayed, *"The LORD is slow to anger, abounding in love and forgiving sin and rebellion"* (Numbers 14:18). The Psalmist urged Israel to, *"Give thanks to the LORD, for he is good. His love endures forever"* (Psalm 136). Time and again the prophets, who warned of severe judgments from God upon Israel and others, followed those warnings with promises of restoration and blessing from benevolent God (e.g. Jeremiah 30 and 31).[1] It is a woefully inadequate and inaccurate depiction of God to portray him as *eternally* committed to dealing with fallen, weak, even rebellious humanity from a posture of unresolved wrath and vengeance. Reading the Bible without appreciating the scope of God's merciful and loving nature can leave one with an incomplete view of God as angry, harsh and violent.

Jesus, whom the Book of Hebrews describes as *"the radiance of God's glory and the exact representation of his being,"* made the matter much clearer. His whole life was a flesh and blood demonstration of what God is really like.[2] He declared by word and example that a New Covenant that would not be hindered by human limitation was being put in place to govern human affairs from his time on. Here are his words: *"My command is this: Love each other as I have loved you. Greater love has no one than this, that he lay down his life for his friends"* (John 15:12-13). Also, *"You have heard that it was said, 'Eye for eye, and tooth for tooth.'* **But I tell you**, *do not resist an evil person. If someone strikes you on the right cheek, turn to him the other also. And if someone wants to sue you and take your tunic, let him have your cloak as well. If someone forces you to go one mile, go with him two miles. Give to the one who asks you, and do not turn away from the one who wants to borrow from you. You have heard that it was said, 'Love your neighbor and hate your enemy.'* **But I tell you**: *Love your enemies and pray for those who persecute you, that you may be sons of your Father in heaven.* **He causes his sun to rise on the evil and the good, and sends rain on the righteous and the unrighteous**" (Matthew 5:38-45 emphasis mine). "Evil and good", "righteous and unrighteous", God includes us all in his loving grace and mercy, and as we become more secure in our restored identity as God's children, we will learn to do the same.

Jesus talked the talk and walked the walk. He voluntarily submitted himself to be betrayed to his enemies, abandoned by his friends, to be despised, rejected, falsely accused, mocked, brutally beaten, tortured and executed, though he had done nothing wrong. He did not fight back; he did not resist; he did not defend himself; and he bore no grudge against his abusers. In the most intense moment of his agony he prayed, *"Father, forgive them, for they do not know what they are doing"* (Luke 23:34). It is difficult for me to imagine that Jesus had an expectation other than his *Abba* would answer that prayer.

If Jesus had thought for a moment that his Heavenly Father was the vindictive, wrathful God that our misunderstandings of the biblical record sometimes make him out to be, I doubt if he would have *"endured the cross, scorning its shame"* (Hebrews 12:2). It surely would have been very disheartening to him if he had believed that, in spite all of his best efforts, the majority of people weren't going to receive any benefit from his sacrifice and would be excluded from heaven and tossed into the flames of an *eternal* hell. But, he had a far different perspective on his Heavenly Father and where his suffering would take him. He saw *"joy set before him..."* when he would be seated *"at the right hand of God"* (Heb. 12:2), *"where he would wait for his enemies to be made his footstool"* (Hebrews 10:13)— he saw his mission accomplished!

Yes, one can sense the shock and momentary alarm it caused Jesus when our sin worked its wages of death upon him. Never before had he experienced anything like that, and in genuine terror he cried out, *"My God, my God, why have you forsaken me?"* But, even in that darkest shadow of death, Jesus said with his last breath, *"Father, into your hands I commit my spirit,"* indicating that, to the very end, he felt a connection to his Heavenly Father.

How could he do this? How could Jesus endure the agonies of the cross and seek God's forgiveness for those who were inflicting upon him the cruelest injustice any human being has ever known?

First, he was compelled by divine love that *"keeps no record of wrongs"* (I Corinthians 13:5). It is the same love that *"God has poured out... into our hearts by the Holy Spirit, whom he has given us"*, and which keeps hope alive in us as we run the gauntlet of heartaches and struggles of life (Romans 5:4-5). Second, as already noted, he understood and sympathized with the weaknesses of his oppressors.

Third, he knew his future was secure in God. Quoting from Psalm 16, Peter explained Jesus' perspective: *"Therefore my heart is glad and my tongue rejoices; my body also will live in hope, because you will not abandon me to the grave, nor will you let your Holy One see decay. You have made known to me the paths of life; you will fill me with joy in your presence"* (Acts 2:26-28). Having learned obedience through his suffering, Jesus was able to endure his darkest moments with the assurance that he was going to come out on the other side of it with joy in God's presence. By God's grace we have similar high expectations for our own future.

As we think of how to follow Jesus' example in our circumstances, having a window broken by a golf ball obviously does not fall into the same category as being the victim of a violent rape or brutal murder. There is no way I would infer that one on the receiving end of such heinous crimes should be expected to not *feel* a deep, visceral desire for at least equivalent retribution. Any one of us would. It is at this point that the *"message of the cross"* (I Corinthians 1:18), and *"the message of reconciliation"* (2 Corinthians 5:19b) are so critically important. Understanding and believing in the full impact of the cross of Christ on matters of injustice and the corresponding suffering they cause, empowers me to excuse myself from participating in a futile, vengeance-driven reaction to being mistreated by others. God identified with and took into his being all injustices (past, present, and future) when Christ was nailed to the cross. No one knows better than God what it feels like to be on the receiving end of injustice and brutality. And no one other than God is qualified to respond to injustice in an unbiased and just way.

Being assured that no inequity escapes his notice and response, I do not have to be enticed into the trap of taking revenge. When I break the chain of vengeance, I am in no way allowing evildoers to get away with their deeds. Actually, just the opposite is true. *"It is mine to avenge; I will repay," says the Lord."*[3] None of us who have wrongly treated another person gets away with it. God took personal oversight of it in Christ, and continues to deal with it as he *"corrects, molds, or perfects the mental faculties or moral character"* (Webster) of every one of us until his reconciling embrace works its way into our hearts and minds.[4]

Everyone who is "touched" by the message of the cross and the saving power it releases in us has been "adopted" into the process that transforms each one into a messenger of reconciliation. The Reconciler himself transforms us into reconcilers who are then teamed up with him to extend his inclusive embrace to all. Drawing upon the inner strength of divine love that is *"poured out...into our hearts by the Holy Spirit, whom he has given us"* (Romans 5:5), we are empowered to endure suffering, grow in character and rejoice in hope (Romans 5:1-5). *"My command is this: Love each other as I have loved you,"* Jesus instructed (John 15:12). The Holy Spirit at work in us makes this possible.

The Spirit is such a complete resource that he even gives us the capacity to love our enemies. Sadly, we fumble at drawing upon this resource as we could, which is one of the human weaknesses that garner God's sympathy. But graciously, with patient, kind, persevering love, God brings us along toward his unfailing objective (I Corinthians 13:4-8), disciplining us for our good as necessary, because, *"Love never fails."*[5] As more and more are added to the Reconciler's love team, there will be increasing evidence that evil is being overcome by good (Romans 12:21).

I do not pretend it is easy. We sometimes groan under the burden of it all.[6] It's a matter of constantly reminding ourselves that everyone, including the one who is wronging us, has weaknesses with which we, and more importantly God, can sympathize. As an elementary school child, my daughter who was being belittled by a classmate astutely observed, "Mommy, people who hurt, hurt others, don't they?" We all exhibit our pain and weaknesses in different ways. We're all struggling with the same basic disappointments, injustices and evils. Paul underscored this reality when he wrote, *"You, therefore have no excuse, you who pass judgment on someone else, for at whatever point you judge the other, you are condemning yourself, because you who pass judgment do the same things"* (Romans 2:1).

The more I lash out in vengeful anger at someone who is mistreating me, the deeper the hole of self-condemnation I dig for myself. Anger invites anger. Contempt breeds contempt. Bitterness destroys. Now *that* is hell! But once I come to terms with the fact that, because of my own weaknesses, I am not entitled to make any claim to moral superiority over another, it becomes a smaller step to put myself in the other person's shoes. I am then able to join Christ in sympathizing with the weaknesses of others.

I hasten to add that there is a vast difference between sympathizing with the weaknesses behind acts of injustice and pretending a wrong was not done. A sympathetic response should not bypass the essential work of confession of wrongdoing and repentance. God's loving discipline in our lives ultimately leads everyone to bow in confession of Christ's Lordship and, by implication, admit our wrongdoings. We will all have to face up to our sins of mistreating others. Because of his love, correction is given so *"that we may share in his holiness. No discipline seems pleasant at the time, but painful. Later on, however, it produces a harvest of righteousness and peace for those who have been trained by it"* (Hebrews 12:10-11)

Once we are convinced that justice sought through personal revenge, outbursts of anger, and reciprocal mistreatment of others neither satisfies nor offers any lasting solutions, we are ready to explore the alternative. Empowered by God's unstoppable love, and equipped with the perspective that comes from sympathizing with the weaknesses of others, we are able to take proactive steps toward a brighter future. Jesus endured the cross because he saw joy beyond it. He saw his cause vindicated, justice accomplished, and those he sought to seek and save included in God's redemptive grace. Likewise, if we have any confidence at all in God's ability to redeem his creation and renew "all things" (Matthew 19:28), we, too, have the capacity to endure what Paul described as *"light and momentary troubles"* (II Corinthians 4:17). We know justice will prevail. The day is coming when no one will feel that others got away with something they should not have. We'll finally appreciate the power of the cross of Christ and be fully embraced in the reconciling love of God.

Of course, that day is not yet here. We are threatened daily by serious evil. Certainly we still need the services of law enforcement, the courts, and keepers of the peace. The Scriptures tell us that God assigns governing authorities to *"bring punishment on wrongdoers"* (Romans 12:4). But, as the authorities go about protecting us and punishing wrongdoers, the rest of us can put our energies into loving as God loves, sympathizing with the weaknesses of offenders, and looking forward to the completion of God's justice for them, as well as for ourselves. We can mercifully pray as Jesus prayed, "Father, forgive them." We can seek God's help to gain what it takes to love our enemies. We do not have to give ourselves over to intolerance, hatred and hostility, but can take seriously our role as ambassadors of reconciliation (II Corinthians 5:20).

The fact is that the vengefulness we most commonly feel toward others typically isn't the result of physical acts of terror or criminal assault against us. Most of it comes from the emotional pain of being misjudged, misunderstood, criticized, insulted or slighted in some way. The compounding of the hurts we develop over these bitternesses and unresolved conflicts continue to fester and eventually bursts, often times leading us to angrily lash out at others, who then feel mistreated or "assaulted" by us. This is an evil and hellish cycle of existence from which God seeks to save us. The power of good, resident in the cross and the message of reconciliation, are going to overcome this evil in the end. Thus it is written: *"Do not be overcome by evil, but overcome evil with good"* (Romans 12:21).

8

MINISTERS

~

"The church is people, equipped to serve,
meeting needs everywhere in Jesus' name."
— *Love, Acceptance and Forgiveness*, Jerry Cook;
Regal Books, 1979

"Amy" was a caregiver to her very core. The patients at the assisted living facility where she worked knew it and loved her for it. They knew it in the tender way she bathed them. They knew it from the cheerful calling of their individual names each day as she did her rounds. They knew it when she chose to have her new baby dedicated at the facility so they all could be a part of it. They knew it from the special little gifts she would buy them out of her meager paycheck. And, most of all, they knew it by the way she would stay well beyond her shift to voluntarily be with patients who were terminally ill and lingering at death's door. On her own time, she would stay long hours into the night to hold the hands of those whose families could not be present. Sometimes she would sing their favorite hymn or read to them one of their favorite passages from the Bible.

"No one should ever have to die alone," Amy would say as she grieved the loss of each one.

With the same passion she poured her heart into the demands of being a young wife and mother. As many young moms do, she lived on the edge of exhaustion most of time. Amy, along with her husband, "Chris", also made it a priority to be faithful to the little start-up church that was meeting in rented theater space nearby. It was a struggle to pack up the baby to attend midweek services on those frozen winter nights in the northern state where they lived. But they liked their young pastor and wanted only success for the church he was starting. Devotedly they were in attendance Wednesdays and Sundays. They even volunteered. Chris led worship and Amy worked in the nursery and participated in the drama ministry when she could. This added rehearsals and staff meetings to their already overloaded schedule.

From time to time, Amy would have to miss a service or a practice at church, because one can't foresee when a patient in a nursing facility will take a turn for the worse and begin the countdown of their final hours. She regretted it, but in her mind there was no question where she was needed the most—God wanted her holding the hand of a dying senior citizen while softly singing his or her favorite hymn so they could slip into eternity as peacefully as possible. Frankly, it just seemed not as important to be at a drama practice where the young adults of the drama team spent most of the time kidding around and telling jokes.

Amy understood the annoyance with her absence that would be subtly communicated by the pastor. She already felt guilty when she was unable to follow through with a commitment, so she would take it to heart when he would indirectly make comments about how essential it was that they, "all make the sacrifices necessary to minister with excellence for Jesus' sake." Amy had been raised to regard the church schedule as a top priority. One of her memory verses as a child had been Hebrews 10:25 - *Let us not give up meeting together, as some are in the habit of doing, but let us encourage one another—and all the more as you see the Day approaching.* And so she began to wonder if maybe she shouldn't give up her job so it wouldn't get in the way of "serving the Lord."

This continued for a couple of years as the little church, struggling to grow, called upon the handful of couples and college students who were the regulars to give more and more of their time and money. Denominational start-up funds were going to be running out soon and the young pastor felt a tremendous burden to connect with the "spiritual seekers" who hadn't yet sought out his church. It was decided that the only way to make the church grow was to do more of what they had been doing, only better. This meant more meetings to plan and more rehearsals to get it right. Some weeks Amy and Chris felt pressured to be involved in the "ministry" four and five nights a week in addition to working full time jobs and raising an infant son who had significant health challenges. They were also committed to building relationships with some co-workers at their jobs who didn't attend church, relationships which had led to some interesting conversations about God. Their new friends were curious about Chris and Amy's faith and wanted to know more, so were invited to accompany them to church services on several occasions. A couple of their friends had come along a time or two, but they had no enthusiasm for returning—one made a comment about it being so "churchy."

Hearing that Chris and Amy (and some of the other regular church attendees) had inroads with some "unchurched" people, the pastor encouraged his church regulars to invite their friends into their homes for small group Bible studies that he or a trusted Bible teacher in the church were eager to lead. Chris suggested that he and Amy preferred to lead the friends they were hosting in their own home in the Bible discussions, an idea that was quickly rejected by the pastor, "because we need to make sure we're teaching the right things and are all on the same page." He felt that only he and his loyal Bible teaching member were trustworthy enough to maintain the necessary quality control.

Weary and discouraged, Amy and Chris began to lose motivation for the ministry. They began to back out of some of the church activities. They felt energized by the care giving and sharing they were doing at their jobs, but church was becoming a real drag. When it was time to organize the big Fourth of July seeker event for their church, Amy said she just couldn't do it, and when pressured to take a certain responsibility, she declined. The following Sunday the pastor preached a particularly strong message about taking up the cross and following Jesus. With urgent tones and furrowed brow he warned his congregation that unless they all "sold out to Jesus" God would not be able to bless the church. Afterwards, he cornered Amy and reminded her that, because of her strong church background, it was important for her to set an example for others by "putting the ministry first."

Amy and Chris left that church and now give themselves to being devoted parents, caregivers and friends.

Amy and Chris are the victims of a deeply ingrained church culture that diminishes church attendees as individuals and reduces them to mere cogs in a greater ecclesiastical machine. Their story reveals one of the major flaws of church life that is perpetuated by so many local churches. It is a flaw that is born of poor theology, a defective leadership model, and a misunderstanding of what constitutes Christian ministry—and it is nothing new.

The first Christians in Jerusalem tenaciously held onto their temple-centered routine even though they knew that Christ's death and the tearing of the curtain to the Holy of Holies made the temple obsolete as the *holy center* of religious life (Mt. 27:51; Mk. 15:38; Lk. 23:45). Jesus had told them to *get power and go* from Jerusalem (Acts 1:8), but after getting the power, they stayed in Jerusalem hanging around the temple for several years (Acts 2:46; Acts 8:1). Although Jesus had predicted the destruction of the Jerusalem temple and that the scattering of his followers would bring an end to the building-centered worship model of the Old Covenant (Matthew 24), early Christians continued to act as if most of the activities associated with service to God were linked to this "worship center", and only moved out when forced to by persecution. Once scattered, some, like the Apostle Paul, appeared to be grasping the concept and taught: *"The God who made the world and everything in it is the Lord of heaven and earth and does not live in temples built by hands. And he is not served by human hands, as if he needed anything, because he himself gives all men life and breath and everything else"* (Acts 17:24-25). But, even Paul continued to carry on with temple customs whenever he was in Jerusalem. Today, we continue to have a hard time unhooking our relationship with God from architecture and holy men.

After the destruction of Jerusalem in 70 AD, and the persecution of Christians and Jews that ensued, Christians wanting to meet together had to do so "underground" in caves and catacombs. So we have to be sympathetic toward their longing to have their own "houses of worship" when Christianity finally came to the forefront in the Roman Empire. However, savvy politicians and religious leaders quickly recognized that the construction of a cathedral, basilica or village church went a long way toward establishing social order and solidifying their positions of power. It became fashionable for nobles and feudal lords to build church buildings, some of them very ornate and elaborate, to prove their piety and curry favor with the peasants and the pope. Those in power expected that the people's gratitude for the generosity of their benefactor would be shown by regular participation in the activities that went on there and loyalty to the clergy assigned to that parish.

The clergy also developed ways of obligating the people. Once the populace became convinced that "officially recognized" clergy would dispense the necessary salvation and favor of God they so desired only at certain facilities, they were much easier to control. Martin Luther emphasized the *priesthood of all believers* and *sola scriptura* as a reaction against many of these controlling manipulations of the populace going on in his day.[1] Luther protested against the corrupt sale of "indulgences" (forgiveness or certain blessings that were sold for profit) by the parish priests for their own personal gain or to fill the coffers of the church. He also declared that it was the Scriptures, not the church or the clergy, that were to be the foremost authority governing the faith walk of each individual believer. As Luther saw it, *the just shall live by faith*,[2] rather than through the intermediary role of "officially certified" clergy who had postured themselves so people had to do as they said to be "right with God." The Protestants, as the reformers who took up Luther's cause later came to be known, didn't fully learn the lesson either. A group of them known as The Puritans, who came to America in quest of religious freedom and economic opportunity, are said to have sent out men during church meeting times that would go from house to house and write down the names of anyone found not in attendance at the meeting so they could be publicly disciplined and rebuked.[3] Enforcement tactics may be different today, but many contemporary pastors harbor the same attitude toward absentees.

For all the convenience that a church building offers (e.g., protection from the elements, an established central meeting place), it is almost impossible, once built, to justify its existence and physically maintain it without, in some way, obligating people to it. Working in tandem with this reality, pastors, priests and career religionists know that church buildings accommodate larger groups of people than, say, a neighbor's living room or a table at a coffee shop. Larger groups of people that gather at a building for the religious services being offered give more money when the plate is passed. Bigger offerings usually lead to better salaries for the religious professionals who then, not surprisingly, become accustomed to a certain standard of living. Even in start-up churches, if they have the long-range goal of becoming "self-sustaining" (having their own facility with adequate income for the programs and staff), the need to obligate people is immediate, as Chris and Amy discovered. More people, more building, more income, more programs, more people, more building, more income… it leads to an institutional vortex that sucks the life out of many.

All the while, the foundational theological principle gets lost. God does not dwell in buildings (or programs) *per se*, and our primary mission in life as Christians is not to gather into buildings, but to go out into the world in Jesus' name. For Christians in one locale to have a functional place where they can meet in greater numbers from time to time is not a bad thing—buildings can be useful tools. But, declaring these buildings to be "holy sanctuaries" where the people *must* gather if they want to serve and experience God is poor theology and an insidious form of spiritual abuse. Until church leaders approach their service to fellow Christ-followers with the goal of working themselves out of a "job" by equipping and empowering people like Chris and Amy to *go* and have maximum impact in their relational networks, not much is going to change. So long as we continue to try to obligate people to orbit their spiritual lives around church buildings and religious professionals, we can expect another generation of potentially world-changing Christ-followers to fall far short of what could be.

Wise local church leaders who understand it is their role to *"prepare God's people for works of service,"* as Paul instructed the Ephesians (4:12), will not be looking for ways to corral and harness the 'Chrises and Amys' they encounter. Instead, they will look for ways to come alongside them, observe their personal strengths and passions, recognize and complement their spiritual gifts, and encourage them to be high impact Christ-followers in their homes, neighborhoods, and workplaces.

Ray,[4] the acclaimed biopic of the late great singer, Ray Charles, portrayed a life-altering scene from his childhood. Ray Charles Robinson started going blind at the age of seven. His poor, single-parent mother set about to teach him self-reliance. "Don't let nothing or nobody turn you into a cripple," she exhorted him repeatedly. As he had all but lost his sight, she informed him that he would have to learn how to get around on his own. Her plan to prepare him for the hard road ahead was to first teach him how to find his way and how to do things for himself, then she would watch him as he attempted each new lesson to make sure he accomplished it satisfactorily and safely, and finally, she cautioned him, she would require him to be on his own. Knowing that they were dependent upon the meager income she was able to earn as a sharecropper and washwoman, she knew she had to teach him in a short period of time how to get along by himself. When she eventually recognized that she had taught him all she could, she sent him away to a school for the blind, suppressing her motherly desire to keep her only living child close by. As the movie portrays, Ray Charles overcame many life challenges because of the character his mother instilled in him by compelling him to let go of her apron strings. She empowered him for success.

In a similar vein, Paul wrote to the Philippians: *"Therefore, my dear friends, as you have always obeyed—not only in my presence, but now much more in my absence—continue to work out your salvation with fear and trembling, for it is God who works in you to will and to act according to his good purpose* (Philippians 2:12-13). Similarly, the writer to the Hebrews urged: *"Therefore let us leave the elementary teachings about Christ and go on to maturity..."* (Hebrews 6:1). Unlike Ray Charles' mother and Paul, too many spiritual leaders (and the institutions they lead) seek to foster dependency in their "offspring". It is all too threatening for those who need to be needed (a characteristic of many pastors) to think of their followers as being able to function just fine without them. So, we have taught our members to look to us for the "good" prayers, the best explanations of the Scriptures, and the godliest solutions to their problems. We have, in essence, taught them that if they will stay in attendance at church services, sit at our feet as we preach and teach from impressive podiums, and direct their focus (and money) toward us, *we* will work out their salvation for them.

In contrast, consider what Jesus did with his own disciples. He thrust them into a globally expanding ministry without any "official" church membership, having never attended Sunday school, having no denominational credentials, no seminary degrees, and having never read the New Testament. He even left them on their own *before* the Holy Spirit was given to comfort and guide them! And, in less than a generation they turned their world upside down. The Chris and Amys we all know will do the same if we unleash them from institutional constraints and bless them in their going.

9

CHURCH CONSUMERS

"And all the believers met together constantly and shared everything they had. They sold their possessions and shared the proceeds with those in need. They worshiped together at the Temple each day, met in homes for the Lord's Supper, and shared their meals with great joy and generosity— all the while praising God and enjoying the goodwill of all the people. And each day the Lord added to their group those who were being saved."
Acts 2:44-47

"Pastor Steve," one of the church elders said, "I think we need to put some advertising on the radio. I was listening to Swindoll today and I heard "First Church's" radio ad. It sure was slick! We need to do that." He went on to say, "I've taken the liberty of making a couple of calls and talking to the station manager at "WKKK", the local Christian radio station, and she said she'd make us a deal if we bought a package of ads." Even though I had been struggling with the notion of churches advertising on Christian formatted radio stations, I was pleased with the elder's initiative and didn't want to 'rain on his parade', so I half-heartedly responded, "I'll put it on the agenda for the next elders meeting." I had learned I could hide indecision and pass the buck that way.

A few days later I was in my study preparing my weekly Bible study when there was a knock on the open door. (It was my custom to keep the door open because I wanted my congregants to see their pastor as available and approachable.) Before I had the chance to look up, 'Janice' interrupted, "Pastor, I need to talk to you for a few minutes." I never could understand why these impromptu urgent meetings always had to happen when I was deep in study. Why was it no one ever felt urgency to meet with me when I was procrastinating and wasting time playing computer games on my office computer?

Janice, along with her husband, 'Jerry', had attended the church regularly for a couple of years. They gave generously and had lots of suggestions about how we should do things. We had implemented some of their suggestions, but I had grown a little weary of the ongoing critique and comparisons of our church with the two previous churches they had attended. Her tone let me know that this was not going to be an uplifting conversation. It brought to mind the comment of one of the other local pastors at the ministerial association meeting I'd attended the week before... "Have any of you ever noticed how many phone calls or requests for appointments you get involve some problem or bad news?" he asked. "I'm getting to the place that every time the phone rings at my house I get a sinking feeling," he continued. The rest of us sitting at the table nodded our heads in agreement. "And more often than not it is just some petty complaint," one of the other pastors added. "Pastoring would be a great line of work if it weren't for the people," I had chimed in, trying to be witty with the others.

Before I could get up from my chair and come out from behind my desk, Janice had proceeded into my study and seated herself in the chair I normally sat in when meeting with people in my office. Since we had met several times before, she must have decided we needed a new seating arrangement; rather than asking her to move, I took the seat on the sofa.

"What's up?" I asked her, wanting to get straight to the point. "Jerry and I have been doing a lot of talking and praying about something and feel like God has led us to a decision," she replied. "Oh great," I thought, "God, Jerry and Janice are going to gang up on me." (I used to wonder where people get the idea of spiritualizing what they have to say and hiding behind God until I started listening to tapes of my sermons. They had learned it from pastors like me!) She continued, "We've been struggling lately with the church. We've been feeling like we need something more. We're not getting fed like when we first came here. I know you've been trying to lead the church toward community involvement and a deeper concern for single moms, street kids, and the poor, but we need to be fed the Word. What about *our* needs? Whatever happened to *'Teaching God's Word in a Practical and Relevant Way'* as it states under the logo in the bulletin? It seems to us like you've let all this compassion stuff get in the way of feeding the flock the meat of the Scriptures."

She went on about good worship songs and hymns we didn't sing anymore and something about some fundraiser she didn't like. But to be honest with you, I had stopped paying attention about the time she uttered the words, "not getting fed." Experience had taught me these are code words for "goodbye, we're outta here." I tuned back in to what she was saying just in time to hear her comment that they were "feeling led" to go to "First Church". "We heard their radio spots and we're going to go check them out."

Every pastor in every church has had similar conversations with someone they thought was one of their faithful regulars. Although this is a fictionalized account, it is based upon many similar conversations and events I have been a part of through my years as a pastor. With experience, a pastor isn't caught by surprise as much as in the early years, but it always disappoints and always feels like personal rejection when folks leave a congregation. At least Janice was decent and courageous enough to let me know they were leaving; more often than not people simply "disappear" from a congregation, and when the pastor, or somebody important doesn't call them right away to ask why, they add, "not caring about us," to their list of gripes about the church.

One afternoon I decided to take one of my drives around my city. I often take drives to think, meditate and pray. God and I have had some awesome conversations while I take in the scenery, listen to "golden oldies" or a favorite CD, and go to who-knows-where. I like to get onto streets I've never been on before and see where they take me. Somehow it's relaxing.

As I drove along that afternoon, I began to notice the churches I was passing. Many of them had banners and signs out in front to be viewed by passersby. Several advertised a "Contemporary Service." Others were promoting programs for kids. A couple of them invited visitors to their coffee bar in the foyer. There were an assortment of sermon topics and programs relating to successful marriages, good parenting or management of personal finances on display. One church had a sign that unapologetically declared, "Fundamental, Dispensational, King James Bible, Nondenominational." I remembered the sign in front of my own church that had recently advertised a Bible curriculum conference we had hosted. Church after church offered some enticement to come in and get what they were offering.

As I was contemplating all I was observing, I reflected back to the church planting training I had received several years earlier. One of the things we spent a great deal of time on was developing what the trainer called our "shtick". Each prospective church planter had to be able to communicate a catchy purpose statement that was appropriate to our "target audience". We thought we were being real clever when we put the phrase "*A Church for People Who Don't Like Church*" on our letterhead. It was our *shtick*, our gimmick. Someone once asked my wife, "What happens if I come to your church and start liking it?" She quick-wittedly responded, "Then you'll have to leave, because this is a church for people who don't like church." Hearing of that conversation, however, robbed me of some of my enthusiasm for the phrase. The point is that, as a pastor, I had been just as guilty as anyone of promoting my church to a target audience and offering goods and services that would entice others to "check them out," as Janice had put it about "First Church". And here I was preparing to go to a church board meeting where we would discuss purchasing advertising on a radio station with a majority of their audience already churchgoers!

It was a breakthrough moment for me when I realized that Janice and Jerry and others I could name who, through the years, had left my church to go to another (or left another church to come to mine) were only doing what we have trained them to do. We have turned them into sophisticated church consumers. The more and better programs we offered, the more of our attendees' needs we promised to meet, the greater we hoped would be our market share. As soon as life circumstances changed, or feelings got hurt, or boredom set in, the church down the street or across town was ready to "close the deal with them" on better products. Good consumers that most Americans are, we have learned that the customer is always right. Demand service and expect results. If this "shop" won't do it, another one will. Forget old-fashioned notions of brand loyalty. The moment we pastors and church leaders hitched our wagon to 'church as a growth industry' and made it all about meeting the needs of our customers, we guaranteed many knocks on our study doors from folks feeling like they weren't getting fed.

Am I suggesting that churches should not advertise, not try to minister to felt needs, nor offer the best programs and music possible? Am I suggesting that churches should limit themselves to prayer, preaching and potlucks? Absolutely not! I am wholeheartedly in favor of Christians organizing themselves to care for one another, entertain one another, celebrate God's blessings together, teach each others' kids, deal with addiction issues, discuss the Bible, learn about healthy marriages, and etc. And by all means invite family, friends and neighbors to come along with you.

My concern is that, whether ours is a mega-church or a small congregation, the mission is not to build our church institution. It is my observation that, as soon as "churches" structure things in such a way that they are dependent upon certain levels of income and expected commitments of time from a sustainable or growing "membership" base, they will find themselves under pressure to try and capture a greater share of the market. We then measure our *success* by counting the number of cars in the parking lot, the number of people sitting in rows looking at the back of someone's head on Sunday morning, and the amount of money contributed in this week's offerings. Since just about every church in America is in this predicament, it is easy to see why most church "growth" tends to be transfer growth – people who already think of themselves as Christians going from one church to the next feeding on the buffet of church programs that appeal to them. We may say we're about evangelism, but our programming and budget priorities betray us. Most of our effort and money is expended on servicing already "churched" people.

What pastor or active church member has time to give to the often painstakingly slow and frustrating work of relational evangelism? It's too inefficient and too slow to go through the process of befriending a person, building trust, earning the right to be welcomed into their life, and prayerfully observing the work of the Holy Spirit nurturing that person toward spiritual health. The busy church worker finds he is caught in an institutional grinder that demands increasing amounts of personal time and resources. No wonder there is a direct correlation between the length of time a person has been an active church member and the declining number of friends they will have outside of the church. Unless someone shows promise of joining his or her church, the "sold-out" churchgoer will feel there is no time to spare for agendaless socializing with someone outside their church circle.

Growing churches must invest more and more time and resources into promoting the church with concerts, patriotic rallies, prophecy seminars, and the like; and many advertise them on "Christian"[1] radio stations. Such aggressive programming can create a synergy that results in people with no church home finding a connection to a church. The sad truth, however, is that this consumer-driven system often also produces the "toxic waste" of burned out leaders, church-damaged Christians, and growing ranks of church-hoppers who go from church to church with an entitlement attitude demanding that whatever church they are currently attending keep them fed with inspirational formats to meet their every spiritual, fellowship, and entertainment need.

Though it may seem so, I am not on a crusade against growing churches and quality church programming. Some of my family and best friends are pastors of large churches, which I attend from time to time. I worry about some of their schedules and stress loads, but I would never say they weren't 'called' to do what they are doing, nor attempt to dissuade them from it. But for my part, I had to give it up.

When I resigned from my last church, I had come to the place where I just couldn't give myself to "doing consumer church" any longer. Because I have great confidence in God's grace and intention to seek and save all that are "lost", I am not under any pressure to get people to go to church as if their eternal salvation depended upon it. Absent this pressure, I am free to simply love God and love people. Some of the people I meet become friends with whom I can share God's reconciling love. We enjoy getting together and talking about it. Sometimes we discuss the Bible. Sometimes we pray. Sometimes we don't do either. It's relational and spontaneous and for the most part unprogrammed. And, I've noticed that I come away from these get-togethers feeling well fed.

10

HAZARDOUS MOBILITY

"I was born under a wand'ring star. I was born under a wand'ring star. Do I know where hell is? Hell is in 'hello', Heaven is in 'goodbye forever, now it's time to go'..."[1]

I was "born under a wand'ring star". I attended three different elementary schools in three different towns, two different high schools and three different colleges. I have moved 18 times since graduating from college. Sixteen different towns ranging in size from 2700 to over 6 million in population in two different countries have claimed me as a resident. To date, six years is the longest I have remained in one town. I have all the classic symptoms of R. A. D. D. – Residential Attention Deficit Disorder. Only God knows if I was following his sincerely sought guidance in making each move, or if I have merely been a restless soul who can't sit still very long.

Whatever the case, it has been a great ride! I have had a range of experiences and met a broad spectrum of fascinating people. I have been to places remote and exotic, as well as rat-infested and congested. I have seen life from angles many never see it and would like to believe I'm the better for it. Of one thing I am certain; I wouldn't trade any of it for anything. Well, maybe just one thing... authentic, loving community.

When one is as mobile as I have been, it is next to impossible to become connected to others at a level of relationship that I would describe as authentic, loving community. You can have friends, neighbors and colleagues, but *community* is something deeper and longer in developing. If I have ever experienced it at all, it was only briefly, and I unfortunately mishandled it because of that institutional mindset I described previously.

Few will identify with the frequency and geographic displacement of my moves; but many whose lives are characterized by the mobility of hyper-scheduled lives, job stresses, family demands and more, are as *community challenged* as I have been. And, as we have noted, increasing numbers of people who once thought of their local church as their touch point for some semblance of community, are leaving their church with nothing to take its place. As we follow our hearts away from consumer-driven, institutional church models in quest of a simpler yet more life-giving Christian spirituality, we would do well to avoid the hazards of isolation and of "going it alone".

I took a sabbatical from my professional clergy role in the institutional church to ask God and myself some hard questions and to rethink what it means to be a Christ-follower. In the process, I have found two things to be immensely true and important. First, the "abundant life" (KJV) or "full life" (NIV) Jesus said he came to offer (John 10:10) is lived out in the context of relationships. Among the mysteries of the Trinity are the harmony, love and unity that characterize God. Since we are created in God's image, it stands to reason that there is a godlike level of intimacy and oneness that we can enjoy in our earthly relationships. Toward this end, Jesus prayed that his followers would be "one" as he was with the Father, and walk together in love (John 17). Human beings were designed to be interconnected in positive and constructive ways.

The biblical record indicates God deals with families, tribes and nations (groups) as much as with individuals. To illustrate, we need only consider such Bible verses as: *"For as in Adam all die, so in Christ will all be made alive"* (I Corinthians 15:22). Jews, Christians and Muslims alike eagerly embrace being included in these words God spoke to Abraham, *"...all people on earth will be blessed through you"* (Genesis 12:3). Jesus taught, *"When the Son of Man comes in his glory, and all the angels with him, he will sit on his throne in heavenly glory. All the **nations** will be gathered before him..."* (Matthew 25:31-32 emphasis added). Whatever eschatological significance,[2] if any, one may want to read into the parable of the sheep and goats; the conclusion that Jesus is speaking of nations and not individuals is unavoidable. My personal favorite among those verses that indicate God often deals with us in groups is 2 Corinthians 5:19, *"...that God was reconciling the **world** to himself in Christ, not counting men's sins against them."*

Although the common phrase "a personal relationship with Jesus Christ" is nowhere used in the Bible, in no way do I wish to diminish the value of having one's own intimate communion with God. I simply wish to stress the importance of realizing that none of us stands alone. We are all part of a greater *whole* in God's eyes. All the emphasis on "personal decisions" and "personal relationship" and "free moral agency" that flavored my theological upbringing completely slighted the essential truth that God sees us and relates to us in community.

It is precisely for this reason that hospitality is such a big deal (See Appendix). It is critical that an atmosphere conducive to interaction between people be established. Those who offer hospitality are providing immeasurable service to the kingdom of God. I see hospitality as one of the "vital organ" gifts in the Body of Christ. It may not seem all that glamorous, but we simply can't survive without it (I Corinthians 12).

For a couple of years, my family and I resided in Mexico where we served in the denominational mission. Among the many things I love about the Hispanic people is that they are so hospitable. In the two years we resided there, having occasion to travel and be a guest from Tijuana in the north to Chetumal in the south, we never found a Mexican home, no matter how simply they lived, where we were unwelcome and were not offered something to eat. As one hostess explained it, "We can always add more water to the soup." I have enchanted memories of staying up well into the tropical nights as we savored tacos or *sopa* with tortillas and an assortment of salsas our hosts insisted we share with them. These were precious times of laughter and bonding that I could kick myself now for not appreciating more fully. It taught me something about community—it takes time; it can't be rushed; and food is often a catalyst. One of the characteristics of the first century Christians was that they *"broke bread in their homes and ate together with glad and sincere hearts"* (Acts 2:46). Many Christians in many parts of the world continue in this vein. We, who have been on the frenetic quest for upward mobility and the acquisition of material things (the pressures from which drive us to hide in our homes with doors locked, curtains drawn, while machines answer our phones), are long overdue to slow down and simplify our lives enough to restore to our routine this vital component of authentic, loving community.

The second thing I have learned is that most genuine life transformation happens within the context of loving relationships wherein honesty is expected and trust is established. Most of us have had the experience of being in the crowd when a great sermon was preached and inspiring music was presented. We sat and listened as our minds were stimulated and our emotions were moved. We all love it when that happens. We walk away momentarily inspired and edified. Seldom, however, do these crowd events result in significant life change. We walk to our cars, return to our regular lives and within days forget what the topic of the sermon was and why we felt so blessed in the moment.

As any participant in a 12-step recovery program will tell us, one can hear all kinds of lectures about the evils of their particular addiction, but until they sit in a room on a regular basis, eye-to-eye with a few others who are also working on their sobriety, admit their powerlessness over their addiction, and make themselves accountable to others, little progress toward recovery is likely to be made. Life transformation happens mostly within the context of significant relationships with a few people.

Many churches today recognize that a small group component is vital to the overall spiritual health of their congregation. Some have undertaken major restructuring endeavors in order to facilitate the small group dynamic in their congregational life. They are insightfully asking themselves what good are crowds if few are being spurred on *"toward love and good deeds"* (Hebrews 10:24)? In the context of these small groups gathering together in homes, restaurants, parks, at the beach and in various meeting rooms, folks nurture the kind of relationships where confidentiality is protected, trust is cultivated, forgiveness is guaranteed, and masks are laid aside. It is in these settings, where two or three (or eight or twelve or even a few more) are gathered in Jesus' name that he promises to show up and make a difference in our lives

(Matthew 18:20). Sure, God is present in the crowd events, too. But life transformation is a *process* that happens best when we let others into our lives to walk beside us, laughing with us when we laugh and crying with us when we cry (Romans 12:15). It takes time; it takes patience; it seldom follows an agenda. And, it surfaces in unplanned moments.

Some of us have had to learn these things the hard way. We read about the success some were having with "cell groups" and decided that would be a neat way to grow our own churches. In typical institutional fashion, we formed committees, trained leaders, recruited host homes, organized into zones, ordered curricula, and announced to our congregations that we'd added another nifty program to their already burdensome church schedule. For many of us it was a disaster – an utter failure. So we rationalized that most North Americans will not respond to the small group format and went back to our old consumer-driven, program-based approaches.

Am I making my point? Authentic, loving community takes time. It can't be rushed. It is organic and must be cultivated. It can't be an add-on to a bunch of religious busyness and be expected to develop into much. I've concluded that getting rid of most of that religious busyness is a good place to start to carve out time in our schedules to build authentic community. It must develop naturally within relationships that exist for reasons of affinity and/or family. It's loving each other and loving our neighbors. It's offering hospitality, eating together and having fun. It's caring and talking and hanging out together and playing together. And when it seems right, praying together and sharing how God is working in our lives. It's including others as we build friendship with them along the way.

For some of us who have been so habituated to institutional, highly structured, professionally led, building-centered Christianity, it feels like we are abandoning the Lord to so simplify our Christian walk. It has been reinforced in our psyche that "good Christians" *go* to church every week so we won't be guilty of forsaking the assembling of ourselves together and so we are properly fed spiritually. Ceasing to follow that routine feels very strange at first and the churchgoers in your family will begin to express concerns about your "backsliding" when they note you aren't going to church regularly as you once did. Those who have the church-is-a-building-with-religious-programs-you-go-to mindset cannot conceive that relaxed, simple conversation going beyond surface banter that results in everyone involved loving God and each other more deeply can be "church".

In his provocative web blog entitled *Detoxing From Church*, Jason Zahariades, shares advice he received from a friend who was well along in the process of making this transition: "Here's a strong statement: most [regular churchgoers] are addicted to church culture. Take away their Sunday service, their Bible studies, prayer meetings, and five-song worship teams and they start having withdrawals quickly. I think that it is a necessary part of this process to have a detox time... I would suggest a time of at least a year of not doing the 'normal' church stuff. For us, during that time of detachment we only did a few things together – ask hard questions and eat. Those were our corporate disciplines." Based upon my recent experience I would concur.

The suggestion that many Christians need to take time off from church in order to "throttle down" their religious lives sufficiently to enable them to enter into and appreciate authentic, loving community, is a threatening idea to institutional Christianity if taken seriously—and my assumption is most institutional leaders aren't taking it seriously. They continue to blame the Devil and the Democrats for the gradual attrition and erosion of cultural influence underway in their institutions, while those who are "leaving the church to become the Church" (Barna) are experiencing and gaining fresh understanding of what Jesus meant when he said: *"For my yoke is easy and my burden is light"* (Matthew 11:30) and, *"...I have come that they may have life, and have it to the full"* (John 10:10). As soon as we learn how to be less mobilized by busyness, constant movement, and the endless quest for more (of what we're not sure), the easier it will become to be a part of a vital community of like-minded people who will spur us on toward God's best—abundant life.

11

I'VE BEEN WONDERING

"The apostles performed many miraculous signs and wonders among the people. And all the believers used to meet together in Solomon's Colonnade."
Acts 5:12

"Signs point the way to something and wonders leave you wondering."
— Jack Hayford

An acquaintance, who in his youth was known neither for his piety nor his scholarship, tells of an incident that occurred at the beginning of one of his Bible college classes. The instructor, known to be a woman of earnest spirituality, opened each class time with the greeting, "The Lord be with you." To which the students would respond, "and with your spirit." She would then say, "Let us pray," and proceed to lead the class in an invocation. It was a routine he had grown accustomed to and followed with bored indifference for the most part.

One day, as the class all bowed their heads and closed their eyes in anticipation of her prayer, what followed was not a prayer but complete silence. Wondering what the delay was, my acquaintance took a peek forward. To his surprise the instructor was no longer standing in front of the class. Opening his eyes fully, he began to search the room for her whereabouts. Only after scanning around the room completely did he notice that the instructor was lying on the floor. The tranquility and bliss on her countenance gave him and the class the distinct impression that she must have "fallen under the power of God." When I questioned him as to how he responded to that development he humorously stated, "A couple of us looked at each other and shrugged our shoulders, then I suggested that the Holy Ghost must have canceled class, and got up from my seat, stepped over her prostrate body in the doorway, exited the classroom and headed to the student lounge to play ping-pong." Others followed. It was later reported that she reclined in that position for nearly an hour, claiming to have been, "slain in the Spirit."[1]

After enjoying the humor of his account, I found myself looking for some rational explanation for such a weird occurrence. It wasn't the first time encountering such phenomena had left me full of questions and skepticism. Reports of these kinds of "spiritual" manifestations always take me back to an incident that happened when I was in the eighth grade.

The founder of the Pentecostal denomination in which my father was an ordained pastor came to our church for a series of revival meetings and to fill the pulpit while my parents were away on a trip. He was revered in our circles as a dynamic leader full of faith and power, having formed a new association (they didn't call themselves a denomination in those days) made up of mostly poor farmers, lumbermen, packinghouse and factory workers in the midst of the Great Depression. These were the days when Pentecostals were looked down upon as those "holy rollers" and "chandelier danglers" from across the railroad tracks – meaning they had wild things going on at the storefronts and little places where they usually met on the poorer side of town. Hardened by societal rejection, full of Pentecostal 'fire' and evangelistic zeal, these 'tongues speakers' went around the country holding tent meetings and starting churches. There was great anticipation in my home church that the founder of our movement, now retired, was coming back to bring the Baptism of the Holy Ghost and other signs and wonders to us again.

My own excitement for the occasion had more to do with the fact that we'd be at church several nights in a row, meaning I'd get to see the girl I had a crush on much more than usual. We had discovered that folks getting filled with the Holy Ghost aren't always paying close attention to the kids, which allowed us ample time to sneak together into the dark classrooms and hidden corners of the building to "make out".

It was not uncommon during such revival meetings for people to stay and pray at the altars or in the prayer room they called the "Upper Room", late into the night. This particular night was no exception and, after my girlfriend had gone home, I went and stood in the doorway of this prayer room to watch the power of God at work as I waited for the family I was staying with to finish their time with God. The sight of people I knew to be regular people, who told jokes, enjoyed potlucks and played softball, lying on the floor speaking in tongues, weeping, shouting and shaking always fascinated me. Even in my cynical and rebellious early teen years, I was respectful when others seemed to be getting something from God. I had prayed to 'get the Holy Ghost' a few times through my childhood but nothing had happened. So I had resigned myself to the fact that these "tarrying meetings," as we called them, worked for others but evidently not for me.

Like a typical 14-year-old boy, with hands stuffed into my pockets, I slouched in the doorway observing all the unusual manifestations. The denomination founder particularly intrigued me as he went from person to person placing his hand on their foreheads and shouting out commands for them to be filled with the Holy Ghost, or be healed, or whatever he felt they needed. As he did this, some would begin to tremble, others would burst into tears, one of my church buddies started speaking in tongues when he was touched, and some would just fall down and lie on the floor. I wasn't feeling anything as I stood there, but "good for them," I thought to myself.

Quite unexpectedly, two of the big elders of the church approached me and said I needed to come into the room and get in on what God was doing. I declined but they wouldn't take no for an answer. They literally grabbed me, one on each arm, and escorted me to a chair in the center of the room. The only way I could have escaped was to make a big scene, tear away from them if I could, and bolt for the door. Out of respect for the founder of our movement and the people who seemed to be getting blessed by God, I chose not to make such a scene. I was trapped! What happened next haunted me for years.

They got the denominational leader's attention and waved him over to lay hands on me. The men who were holding onto me thrust both of my arms into the air. Lifting one's hands into the air was regarded as the correct posture for receiving something from God. I was too humiliated and too befuddled to make eye contact with the leader as he strode toward me, so I just closed my eyes and resigned myself to the fact that he was going to put his hands on my forehead and yell something over me. But he did not just put his hand on my forehead. He forcefully thrust his hand on my head in a fashion more like he was striking a blow, which startled me and caused me to flinch and recoil. Just as I flinched, the men let go of my arms causing me to lose traction and slide out of the metal folding chair. As I quickly tried to recover my posture, I realized that everyone else in the room was shouting, "Glory to God! He's got it!" What exactly I had "gotten" was not clear to me. But if the founder of our denomination and all the key leaders of our church said I got something, who was I to think otherwise? With great uncertainty I gave thanks to God for whatever it was he had given me. I even tried to speak in tongues but eventually decided faked tongues probably don't count for anything.

The reader will understand why, as I progressed through my teen years, I became very skeptical of such goings-on. I began to entertain thoughts that all this tongues speaking, shaking, falling down, and weeping was just hysteria and out-of-control emotionalism. My irreligious friends from school who would accompany me to an occasional service at our church, which was literally on the other side of the railroad tracks, encouraged me in this irreverent thinking. They thought the people of my church were nuts! And, yet, I couldn't help wondering why so many of those otherwise good, intelligent, hardworking people (including my parents) were so convinced it was real.

By the time I enrolled in Bible college several years later, Pentecostalism was gaining wider acceptance. Episcopalian clergy such as Rev. Dennis Bennett, as well as a businessman from Southern California named Demos Shakarian (founder of the Full Gospel Business Men), several nuns and priests at Notre Dame University, and students and faculty at Asbury Seminary (Methodist), along with others worldwide began to speak openly of Holy Spirit experiences similar to those for which the Pentecostals were known. So widespread was this "outpouring" of the Holy Spirit that it became known as the Charismatic Movement.

In the early days of the Charismatic Movement, not everyone in our "classical Pentecostal" circles was excited about the reports of those "mainline liberals" who were receiving the Holy Ghost. After all the tarrying and self-flagellating quests for legalistic holiness through which we had put ourselves to become qualified to get "the Baptism", it didn't seem right that people who wore crucifixes, prayed the Rosary, smoked tobacco, or read out of the Revised Standard Version Bible were getting the "blessing" with ease and in great numbers. Many of the Pentecostal magisterium spoke against the Charismatics. One old-time Pentecostal evangelist who was preaching at a chapel service at my college got so worked up while making an emphatic point about what the "real" Baptism in the Holy Ghost is that he kicked his leg up in the air, jumped around on one leg while shouting out his condemnation of these Holy Ghost interlopers and proceeded to have a heart attack! True story.

About that same time, Katherine Kuhlman, who had gained national attention as a faith healer, came to town at the invitation of our denomination. She had gained celebrity because of reports that many healings and other spiritual phenomena were taking place in her meetings in Pittsburgh. She not only had her own nationally televised program, she had even been a guest of Johnny Carson on NBC's *Tonight Show*. Ushers were needed for her local healing meeting, so several of my fellow students and I volunteered. I had no idea what I had gotten myself into. Two of us with stocky, athletic builds were selected to stand during the entire service at the steps leading up to the stage in the large civic auditorium. I later learned why.

A standing room only crowd of thousands, including many Catholic nuns and priests, along with clergy from a broad spectrum of denominations, were present to see if this aging, frail woman in her flowing white gown would perform any miracles. She spoke with wide eyes and a melodramatic and spooky voice as she raised her billowing white sleeves, looking like an apparition of a wrinkled angel in the spotlight. By the time she reached the climax of her message the atmosphere in the auditorium was electric. I then realized why I had been selected to stand at the front stairs to the stage, and been instructed so emphatically that under no circumstances was I to allow anyone to go up those stairs onto the stage; as she concluded her message, scores of desperate people rushed the stage! The Kuhlman Team was counting on me to physically block their access. Pushing and angry words ensued. I'll never forget one woman, face twisted in contempt, hair up in a bun and holding a big Bible, who shouted at me, "I rebuke you in the name of Jesus!" She had come for a blessing and I was the devil in her way.

Katherine Kuhlman began to call out healings… "There is a person in that seating section being healed of back pain," she would point and say matter of factly. Heads would turn to look in that direction as someone would scream out, jump to their feet and exclaim that it had just happened to them. This went on for quite some time as various individuals with an assortment of ailments claimed to have been healed. From that "healed group", those who passed the screening interview process of Katherine Kuhlman's associates were then escorted to the stage to be interviewed by her at the podium. They would give testimony to what had happened to them and the crowd would celebrate and shout praises to God. Ms. Kuhlman would then place a couple of her frail fingers gently on their foreheads and they would fall down, presumably rendered unable to stand by God's power.

At a certain point she called for all the clergy in the building to get in a line so she could pray over them one at a time. More than a hundred lined up single file to come onto the stage so she could touch their forehead and pronounce a blessing. I knew several of them from my denomination personally. Almost without exception, as she touched them, down they would go some falling forward and others backwards. Before long, clergy were stacked on top of each other like cord wood in a tangle of arms and legs. Her "catchers", the guys who tried to keep the falling ones from hitting their heads on the floor, could not keep up with her. Often, as she touched someone, a catcher would go down, too. It was wild! It became my responsibility to assist each one down the stairs as soon as they had recovered enough to leave the stage. Many of them were staggering like they were drunk.

This went on for quite some time before Ms. Kuhlman finally exited the stage. I took her hand and helped her down the stairs I was still guarding. As it became apparent that she was leaving the stage, hundreds of people, some on crutches or in wheelchairs, rushed forward. The other stocky usher and I, along with two of her assistants, had to lock our arms around Ms. Kuhlman to protect her from the stampede of people desperately wanting to get to her. It took more than half an hour to force our way through that mob to get her safely to her dressing room. All along the way people were pulling at me, shoving, and even hitting me. One young adult woman in a wheelchair, with whom I had made eye contact, took aim and deliberately rammed me in hopes of knocking me out of the way so she could get close enough to be one of the few Katherine Kuhlman was reaching out and touching.

As the last of the crowd left the building, I sat down on one of the concrete steps in front of the Veterans Memorial Auditorium. I was more physically exhausted and bruised than I had ever been after a high school football game. The images of the pain, frustration, and anger that I had seen on the faces of the many desperate people I had forcefully turned away replayed over and over in my mind. The spectacle of all those clergy piled on top of each other left me incredulous. I was deeply saddened, quite angered, and totally perplexed about it all. I bowed my head and prayed the most honest prayer I have ever prayed. "God, what the hell was that?!"

Parishioners in my first pastorate detected my reservations about Pentecostal spiritual phenomena. One dear old sister, convinced I needed to loosen up, came up to me one Sunday before service and let me know she had been "fasting and praying" that I'd be smitten by the power of God and made to "dance in the Spirit." I was not at all amused by her zeal to see me doing a jig around the sanctuary in full view of everyone, and told her in no uncertain terms that if it ever did happen she'd know God had forced me into it, because I had no desire whatsoever to participate in such a spectacle. I was all about doing things in a "fitting and orderly way" (I Corinthians 14:40). To me, that meant virtually no manifestations would be allowed in my church, even though we gave lip service to the Pentecostal traditions.

This style of leadership served me fairly well through my first decade as a pastor. I focused my attention on expository Bible teaching and encouraged those in my congregation who 'needed' overt Pentecostal manifestations to get involved with organizations such as Women's Aglow and Full Gospel Business Men. These organizations met in off site, neutral places like hotel conference rooms once a month or so. They'd bring in a guest speaker, get happy in Jesus, speak in tongues and prophesy then go on about their regular lives. This outlet took the pressure off me to "get Pentecostal" at church.

Then it happened! I wasn't expecting it and had not been seeking for it to happen. As I said, "fitting and orderly" was my priority. It was a routine Sunday evening service—a few songs sung, announcements made, an offering taken, and my teaching concluded. Before dismissing the faithful ones who had ventured out on a Sunday evening, I asked if anyone had a prayer request to be included in the benediction. A hard-working carpenter, who had no business even being there because he was so sick with the flu, asked if we would pray for him. He was hot with fever, watery eyed, hoarse and coughing. I perfunctorily asked those standing near him to gather around him and prepared to lead my usual pastoral prayer for God's healing mercy. As I reached out to put my hand on his shoulder, along with the others who had stepped toward him to agree with me in prayer, a warm flush surged in my body. Before I could even touch him, he lurched backward and wiped out two rows of stacking chairs before landing face up on the floor. My jaw dropped as my mind raced through a series of questions such as: What just happened? Did he get hurt? Were any of our new chairs damaged? And, now what do I do? The Women's Aglow and Full Gospel Business Men members present were giddy with excitement. Within a couple of minutes he got to his feet, fever gone, eyes clear, completely free of symptoms. This wasn't my denomination founder; this wasn't Katherine Kuhlman or some high-powered Charismatic celebrity! This was me – or God, or whatever! Some things just leave you wondering.

These accounts were written to underscore a point I referred to already, but want to expand further. God will not fit into our definitions and formulas. *"How unsearchable his judgments, and his paths beyond tracing out!"* states Romans 11:33. That is not to say God can't be known at all. Creation, the instruction and guidance of the Holy Spirit, and the Scriptures all reveal wonderful things about God. But, at best, our knowledge is incomplete. A subplot in each of the accounts in this chapter is the fact that someone had expectations of outcomes based upon their "knowledge" of God that didn't pan out. In every account, God colored outside of the lines in some fashion. It matters little whether one comes from a 'signs and wonders' friendly or cessasionist dispensational perspective; sometimes God doesn't follow our formulas.

God is a God of mysteries and surprises. I think he likes it that way, and so should we. But we don't. So we undertake strenuous "tower building"[2] projects of speculation and presumption from which we aspire to reach into the heavens and figure out God. We lay the blocks of a clue here, an insight there, an experience here, an assumption there, and the next thing you know we think we've got a pretty good handle on God's ways. Then, along come the apologists inviting us onto their "towers" by seeking to convince us with persuasive arguments, and, *viola!* —an "absolute" is born— "this is the way God is and this is the way God does." Granted, I don't get to decide, but if I did, the propagation of such "absolutes" would be among the greatest sins. For, in my opinion, it is the construction of such "high places" and the insistence that we all bow down there that has done the greatest harm to the human race.

I think we should allow God some privacy. Much like our parents, perhaps God shuts the "bedroom" door once in a while, not because he doesn't love us and is rejecting us, but because there are some things best carried on behind closed doors. A child must learn that about parents— Mommy and Daddy having a private moment is not a cause for alarm, fear and insecurity. In time, the child will understand what's going on in there and be glad about it. A loving home atmosphere engenders a sense of security in children even when Mom and Dad may be out of sight for the moment. Children who are secure in their relationship with parents will be able to let the door remain closed and not stand outside fussing and pounding to get in.

So much of our traditional doctrine has been developed, not from a healthy sense of "okayness" while the door is closed, but by anxious children of God who have yet to realize how safe they really are in God's house. We have built doctrinal high places so we can pound on the door of heaven and demand that God get back in the room we occupy. Uptight about the mysteries of God, we have codified doctrines and rules by which we seek to dispel ambiguity and any sense of loss of control.

Many of us are feeling like we no longer want to be a part of this neurosis. We have grown weary of formulas, liturgies, rules and "principles" that have given the false impression that, for those who have climbed upon this or that particular tower, a door will be opened. Some things about God do leave us wondering, and that should be okay. He'll let us in when he is ready. In the meantime, I am choosing to rest in the security of God's reconciling love through Jesus Christ and to enjoy him forever.

12

TO HELL AND BACK

~

*"... But anyone who says, 'You fool!' will be in
danger of the fire of hell."*
Matthew 5:22

The phone in my study rang as I was putting the finishing touches to the Bible study I was preparing for the Wednesday Bible Study and Prayer service. I picked up the receiver and answered in my best professional clergy tone, "Hello. This is Pastor Rogers." An excited voice on the other end of the line interrupted, "Have you heard the forecast? They're saying it's going to snow in the mountains." It was Cliff, a fellow pastor, good friend and hunting buddy. Cliff only lived a "neighborly" 50 miles away in southern Montana. We had been looking forward to going elk hunting together but it had been an unusually mild autumn, which meant no snow in the mountains. Where we wanted to go, snow was preferred for serious elk hunters. Finally, the weather forecast was promising. Cliff continued, "It sounds like if we leave right after our services tonight we can get up on the mountain, get camp set up and be ready to catch those elk on the move after the storm. What do you say? We can bring our Bibles and work on our Sunday sermons while we wait for the storm to break."

"Count me in," I responded. "I'll get my gear all ready, shorten my Bible study and head your way. Look for me around 9:00 PM."

"Good. I'll have the camping trailer hooked to the Bronco and ready to go as soon as you get here."

Yes, we were fools, as anyone who knows anything about being in the high country during a major snowstorm can attest. We were going to drive through the night without sleep, dragging a 15-foot camping trailer behind a 1967 Bronco into the bull's-eye of a blizzard. Neither of us had any experience in mountain survival. I had grown up in the farmland of Iowa and Cliff was from the west coast. We were both "flatlanders" and relatively new Montana residents. It was around 6:00 AM the next day when we traversed a treeless, sagebrush covered section of mountain plateau and backed the trailer into a sheltering grove of evergreens at about 7500 feet elevation. The first snowflakes were beginning to gently fall. We set up the trailer and crawled into our sleeping bags to sleep and wait out the storm.

We slept until mid-morning and, after downing a hearty breakfast, decided to take a look around to see if we could spot any game. We soon realized the futility of trying to hunt while the wind was howling and visibility was less than a hundred yards because of blowing snow. We returned to our trailer that was protected from the wind by the sheltering trees. By noon, about four inches of snow had accumulated on the pine boughs around our campsite, creating a postcard pretty winter wonderland. We built a campfire and sat outside as we ate our sandwiches for lunch. After lunch, we returned to the warmth of the trailer and spent an hour or so preparing our Sunday sermons before sleepiness beckoned us to take a nap.

The early darkness of a November afternoon in Montana had come when we awoke from our sleep. We took a look outside and were surprised to see how much it had snowed in the last three hours. In our location out of the wind about eight inches of snow had accumulated. The campfire was still smoldering, so we got it going again. It was dark, cold and snowing hard but the glow and warmth of the fire was reassuring. We heated up some stew and ate it while sitting by the fire as the snow continued to steadily fall. Our outer clothing was getting damp from melted snow as we sat there, and when I stepped away from the fire for a minute, I began to feel the cold and shivered a little.

Cliff remembered how hard the wind had been blowing when we had ventured away from the shelter of the campsite earlier in the day. He said he was going to take the Bronco for a quick spin on the forest service road that crossed the open plateau into our grove of trees, while I preferred to stay in camp seeing no reason to venture out in the darkness. I thought he was just bored, but he told me later he had begun to worry when the snow didn't seem to be ending as forecasted. Not ten minutes later headlights reflected off of the snow covered trees as the Bronco came bouncing back toward our camp. After backing in toward the trailer, he jumped out of the Bronco with a look of panic on his face and said, "We've got to get off this mountain now!" While we had slept and lounged around our sheltered camping spot, a raging blizzard had deposited huge drifts that covered the road wherever it was not protected by trees. Cliff had discovered that while we idled away the time, our sense of tranquility was not at all connected to reality. We were in trouble. It was questionable if we were going to be able to get off that mountain, even with chains on all tires of the four-wheel drive Bronco, but we had to try. Quickly, we put on the chains, packed up our gear, hooked up the trailer, and pulled away from the trees into the teeth of the 40 mph wind that was blowing the snow sideways in whiteout conditions. The little thermometer Cliff had mounted on the front of his trailer said it was zero degrees before factoring in the wind chill.

The snow that had collected on our clothes as we put on the chains and hitched up the trailer began to melt inside the Bronco with the heater going full blast. I shivered again as the dampness penetrated another layer of my mostly cotton coat and sweatshirt. With the Bronco in "four low" we crept along at 5 mph guessing where the road was because of the poor visibility. Our hope was that we could bust through the drifts that covered much of that plateau and be able to descend down the switchbacks that snaked through dense timber to the valley floor.

We hadn't gone a quarter of a mile when all of sudden the trailer dropped down on one side and bogged down in about three feet of snow. We had missed a slight turn in the road and the trailer had slipped into a small ditch. Cliff and I agreed that I would try to shovel away some of the snow around the trailer while he attempted to pull it out while it was still hitched to the Bronco. Furiously I pitched shovel full after shovel full of snow as he spun the tires and rocked the Bronco back and forth trying to get unstuck. I was out in the wind and snow the whole time while he had remained in the vehicle where the heater was blowing. We finally ended up unhooking the trailer, hooking the winch cable to the tongue of the trailer, and dragging it out of the ditch to a place where we could hitch it up again. I had spent about 45 minutes out in that wind and cold. My clothes were now soaked through from the combination of perspiration from the exertion of the shoveling and the melting snow. The wind cut through me like a knife as I stood by holding the flashlight as Cliff got the trailer on the hitch again. By the time I got back in the passenger seat I was shaking uncontrollably and having a difficult time putting my words together. I figured as soon as my teeth quit chattering I'd be able to speak more clearly. It never dawned on me that I was going into hypothermia.

Back on the road we inched along toward our valley destination. My shivering had just about subsided when again we hit a drift and the Bronco got "high centered". Progress came to a halt. Attempts to go in reverse were to no avail. For the first time I began to feel genuine fear as I sat in the rig with confused thoughts trying to ponder our next move. Cliff took charge. "We'll take turns shoveling the snow out from under the Bronco and see if we can get traction. I'll unhook again and drive forward to see if I can break a trail through the drift." Reluctantly, I stepped out into the wind and cold with clothing wetter than ever.

Down on our knees, even lying on our bellies, we took turns extending the shovel under the vehicle to remove the snow that had packed in underneath so tight that the wheels could not grab solid ground. Cliff would get in and out of the rig and try to rock it forward and backward as I struggled to stay on task removing the snow. The plan worked, but my shivering returned convulsively. The Bronco visibly settled to the ground as I removed that last shovel full of snow. With the trailer unhooked, Cliff was able to punch through the twenty yards of drift that clogged the road. While he did that, I continued to shovel around the unhooked trailer. It had been two hours since we had broke camp and we had traveled less than two miles.

In all the commotion I had not noticed that the snow was not falling as hard as when we started. Although the wind continued to howl, visibility had improved a bit. Once we broke through that drift, we found ourselves on a windblown stretch of bare road. I huddled as close to the heater vent as I could, my body shaking uncontrollably and teeth chattering. Melting snow had now soaked through my boots and socks. My toes were numb, but we both felt the worst was behind us. I was having a difficult time concentrating as my body pulled whatever warmth it could from my extremities to maintain warmth for my internal organs.

In my confused and morbidly frightened state I saw two things as we headed toward the opposite side of the open plateau. Out of nowhere appeared two eyes reflecting in our headlights. It was a little weasel-like critter that was scurrying around playfully along the edge of the road. It reminded me of a demonic looking imp and I remember thinking, "You can have this place, I'm not going to die up here." Then, as I looked out the frosty side window of the Bronco into the night, way off in the distance I saw a light. The subsiding snowfall and lifting clouds enabled me to see, flickering through the flurries of wind driven snow, what was apparently a yard light from a distant ranch house in the valley. I was concentrating on that light when we plowed into another drift and got stuck again, this time deeper than ever. Once again, I found myself shoveling snow in below zero temperatures with a wind chill factor that was out of sight. Even though we finally extricated ourselves from that drift by unhooking, doing lots of shoveling, and employing the winch on the front of Cliff's Bronco, the snowfield in front of us was so wide and deep we could not go forward. We were literally trapped on top of that mountain.

Surveying the situation Cliff shouted over the sound of the wind, "Let's drive back up the road and park the rig on that bare place we came through. We've got propane for heat that will last a couple of days. We've got plenty of food. Let's give it up and see what it looks like in the morning." His words sounded far off and indistinct as the wind howled through the ice-encrusted hood of my sweatshirt and stocking cap. My gloves were frozen solid around my numb fingers. I could not even feel my feet. I was shaking uncontrollably as I stared at that light that was at least 10 miles away as the crow flies. All I could think about was, if I stay on this mountain tonight I will die. Incoherently, I mumbled that

I had to get off the mountain and I turned to start hiking toward that light in the valley. Cliff would have nothing of it and physically restrained me while he coaxed me to get back in the Bronco. What I didn't know is that between that distant light and where we were standing was a deep canyon with an impassable sheer rock wall. Had he not intervened, I would have been another of those poor hypothermic souls who, rather than seeking shelter wherein they can ride out a storm, panic and wander off into the darkness and cold only to be found frozen to death the next day.

We found a halfway level spot in the road, got into the still-hitched trailer, and lit the burners on the cook stove to get some heat going. I got out of the wet clothes, put on dry ones and crawled into my sleeping bag. Slowly, the shivering subsided and I began to believe that I wouldn't die – that night at least. After we felt like we were warm enough for the time being, we turned off the stove in order to save our propane. We weren't sure how long we were going to be on that mountain. I finally drifted into sleep, completely buried in my sleeping bag with extra blankets piled on top. I awoke the following morning with an urgent need to relieve myself and when I tried to get out of my sleeping bag, I couldn't. The temperature overnight had plummeted to 20 degrees below zero, which had caused the condensation from my breath to form an ice seal at the opening of the sleeping bag as I slept. I was frozen into it, but because of the urgency of the moment I found a way of escape.

Opening the door to the trailer, I was dismayed to see that there were tracks of another vehicle that had passed by ours while we slept. I could tell that they were fresh and heading up the mountain. Unencumbered by a travel trailer and with a higher ground clearance, two guys in a Jeep had been able to break through the drifts and make their way up the mountain to see if any elk were moving after the storm. Cliff and I had lost all enthusiasm for elk hunting and tried to start the Bronco so we could follow the trail they had broken through the drifts as they came up the mountain toward us. The Bronco wouldn't start, but a short while later the guys in the Jeep came back down the mountain and stopped to talk to us. They used their jumper cables to get us started and dragged us with a tow chain through that last drift, which enabled us to finally begin the descent to the valley.

By the time we reached the valley floor, the snow depth was only a couple of inches and the sun was beginning to break through the clouds. I was never so glad to get off a mountain in my life and a deep sense of relief swept over me. Just as I was making a comment about wanting to get out and kiss the ground, we drove over a cattle guard that was across the road at a fence. The bumpiness of the cattle guard caused the snow and ice encrusted trailer hitch to fail; the unhitched trailer slammed into the back of the Bronco breaking out the entire front window of the camper. It was enough to make a couple of preachers swear.

We stopped in the nearest town to patch the broken window with cardboard and duct tape. It was then that we learned the two mountain passes between our location and home were closed and we were stranded 250 miles from home. We went into a café and ordered lunch. Finally, the report came that a lane had been opened on the first pass and traffic was being allowed to proceed. Reports were that the other pass would be open by the time we got there. We were fatigued but truly delighted as we made it through the passes and started on the final leg toward home. It was late afternoon and darkness was again upon us.

Suddenly, we hit a patch of "black ice" on the otherwise dry highway causing the Bronco and trailer to fishtail at 55 mph. I looked out my passenger side window just in time to see the trailer jackknife into my view. To this day, I marvel at how Cliff was able to get everything back under control and continue down the highway. Our trip to "hell" and back ended exactly 48 hours after it began. Experienced outdoorsmen are quick to point out a long list of mistakes we made that led to our predicament. You can be sure Cliff and I learned a bunch from all we went through.

As I have reflected back on that experience, it has occurred to me that in many ways it parallels our spiritual journey, particularly as it relates to matters of death, judgment and salvation.

Folks with no passion for hunting and the outdoors have difficulty relating, but for those of us who have the passion, it is unavoidable. We have to do it. It is in our blood – it's our nature, you might say. Just as human beings are inclined to sin by nature, some of us sinners are inclined to hunt. Spouses of outdoorsmen across the land have watched their loved ones get that "far-away look" in their eyes, toss and turn through sleepless nights, and lose all perspective as opening day of hunting season approaches and the call of the wild overtakes them. So, when my dear wife pleaded with me not to go on that escapade, I didn't want to hear it. Responsibilities, relationships, common sense, and the laws of nature were no deterrent—I was going to do what I was going to do even if there was hell to pay.

Both sin and hypothermia are subtle enemies. Before I could rationally realize what was happening, hypothermia was paying the deadly wages of my many wrong choices. So it is in life, as sin seduces us into willfulness and a blatant disregard of laws and consequences. The hypothermia that nearly killed me took control of me while I was trying to save myself after such disregard, just as our self-directed efforts to extract ourselves from willful sinfulness oftentimes only lead us farther from God. *"The wages of sin is death,"* Paul wrote (Romans 6:23).

The ironic part of the whole story is that "provision" for our warmth and shelter was right there with us the whole time we went through that ordeal. We could have survived on that mountain for weeks if we had to, with the shelter and supplies that trailer contained. But, because of our fear of the unknown and our misguided attempt to save ourselves, we nearly squandered our lives seeking another option. And, not only did I benefit from a personal "savior" when Cliff wouldn't allow me to go wandering off in the night, we both were "saved" when the hunters broke through to us the following morning and led us off the mountain. Still, even though we were saved, some *dangers, toils and snares,* as the stanza from the hymn Amazing Grace puts it. remained to be dealt with as a result of our foolishness. Valuable lessons had to be learned, as I emphasized in Chapter 7, *Discipline For the "Hell" Of It.*

Let's face it, all of us are sin damaged and "naturally" put ourselves on a path of self-destruction through the combination of bad choices and misguided attempts to save ourselves from the consequences of those choices. We feel alienated from God, quite fearful of life's "storms", and panicked by the unknowns of our own mortality. In reaction to this spiritual insecurity we improvise ways to escape and regain control over our destiny. Through religion we try to pound on the door of heaven in the hope that we can get God to shovel us out of our messes. All the while, God is, and has been present extending his loving grace to all who are lost. We are safe and don't even know it until God intervenes and rescues us from ourselves.

13

MONSTERS IN THE CLOSET

~

> *"This is a trustworthy saying that deserves full acceptance (and for this we labor and strive), that we have put our hope in the living God, who is the Savior of all men, and especially of those who believe. Command and teach these things."*
> I Timothy 4:9-11

I once had a discussion with a woman who was very concerned about the fact that I believe Christ's death on the cross included everyone and would ultimately result in the reconciliation of the entire human race. She, like so many of us, had been warned often to watch out for "false" teachers and suspected I might be one. She lived in fear that, at any given time, she was at risk of being deceived and led away from the truth. To suggest that Christ's death and resurrection were sufficient to guarantee salvation for *all* was just too much good news to be true. She felt the need to wake me up to the dangers of misbelieving and reminded me of Paul's warning to Timothy: *"The Spirit clearly says that in later times some will abandon the faith and follow deceiving spirits and things taught by demons. Such teachings come through hypocritical liars, whose consciences have been seared as with a hot iron"* (I Timothy 4:1-2). Although a dear friend, she was worried that I had come under the influence of something taught by demons.

I asked her to continue reading... *"They forbid people to marry and order them to abstain from certain foods, which God created to be received with thanksgiving by those who believe and who know the truth. For everything God created is good, and nothing is to be rejected if it is received with thanksgiving, because it is consecrated by the word of God and prayer"* (I Timothy 4:3-6). I then asked her, "What are these '*things taught by demons*', as Paul described them?" She correctly observed that Paul was describing a form of legalistic asceticism that was creeping into the churches. Some were abandoning simple faith in Christ and were asserting that a harsh celibacy and a restrictive diet were necessary practices for anyone seeking salvation. I also pointed out to her the limiting, controlling attitude of the false teachers, as contrasted with the generosity of God's attitude. *"They forbid,"* but God *"created* [everything] *to be received with thanksgiving,"* wrote Paul.

Although she began to recognize that Paul had a specific teaching in mind, and that it would be taking it out of context to use this passage as a warning to avoid *any* scriptural interpretations different than what one had been taught, she remained unconvinced. I encouraged her to keep reading. *"If you point these things out to the brothers, you will be a good minister of Christ Jesus, brought up in the truths of the faith and of the good teaching that you have followed. Have nothing to do with godless myths and old wives' tales; rather, train yourself to be godly. For physical training is of some value, but godliness has value for all things, holding promise for both the present life and the life to come"* (1 Tim. 4:6-8). I pointed out to her that, Paul, in all of his writings, advocated a godliness that rested *"in the truths of the faith and of the good teaching that you have followed"* (verse 6). The central truth of Paul's teaching is stated most clearly in Ephesians 2:8-9: *"For it is by grace you have been saved, through faith—and this not from yourselves, it is the gift of God— not by works, so that no one can boast."* Paul strenuously objected to any corruption of the *"truths of the faith"* that attached laws and performance issues and made salvation an achievement rather than a gift of grace.

At this point she closed her Bible, realizing that if she were going to change my mind and rein me back into her exclusive and paranoid doctrine she would need a different passage of Scripture. "Wait," I said, "Don't stop there. Read on." She found I Timothy 4 again and picked it up in verse 9. *"This is a trustworthy saying that deserves full acceptance (and for this we labor and strive), that we have put our hope in the living God, who is the Savior of all men, and especially of those who believe. Command and teach these things"* (I Timothy 4:9-11).

As she read verse 10 where Paul asserts that God *is the Savior of **all men**, and especially of those who believe,* she hesitated, her eyes got big and she could barely get the words out of her mouth. She had grown up in the church and been a Christian all of her life. She was the wife of a seminarian and had herself attended seminary, but nobody had ever pointed that out to her. Leaning upon the preceding verses, many of her pastors and teachers (as I also used to do) had sternly warned her to be on alert for deceivers who might trick her into believing something demonically contrived to lure her into deception. But no one had ever once told her that God is the savior of *all* humanity. I ask, who is deceived?

This lady is typical of many sincere and devout Christians today, convinced they are in danger of falling into error at any moment and completely unsure of the power of God's grace. If you want to talk about a deceiving doctrine of demons, no better example can be found than one that minimizes the efficacy of Christ's death for all and reduces us to fear and insecurity in our spiritual journeys. We are so like little children, afraid of shadows, and bogeymen, and monsters that lurk in our dark closets and under our beds, leading us to hide under our covers and imaginations. But God is a God of light and truth, who wants us to have freedom from the fear of the unknown.

One of the foremost of these imagined monsters is the doctrine of eternal hell. It is a doctrine that is rife with superstition, and completely inconsistent with the nature of God as revealed by Jesus Christ.

Some will be quick to point out that Jesus had quite a bit to say about hell. True enough. But did he teach hell as we have imagined and explained it? Did he teach hell as the ultimate exclusion and rejection of "lost" humanity? Did Jesus really want us to understand that for calling someone a "fool" individuals are at risk of being sent to weep and wail and gnash their teeth in the searing heat of *eternal* torment? Did Jesus really want us to understand that God has so subjected himself to human decision-making that if we choose otherwise, even though Christ went to the extraordinary lengths of dying for our sins, God can't save us—or worse, that God could, but won't, save us? I believe there are compelling reasons to reject such notions and, in so doing, to open our hearts and minds to a much clearer understanding of the Scriptures. But first, we have to quit believing in the bogeyman.

We will stop believing in the bogeyman as soon as we realize God is for us and not against us, and nothing within us or on the outside of us can separate us from God's love (Romans 8:31-39). No matter how badly we misconstrue the mysteries of God, or stubbornly ignore wise counsel, or break God's laws and willfully go our own way, God relentlessly searches and rescues (seeks and saves) all who are lost. This, too, is what Jesus taught (Luke 15; 19:10). The shelter of his reconciling love is close to us at all times and he will coax us into it, even when we fail to recognize it or think we have a better plan.

So from where did this imaginary monster called "eternal hell" come? It depends on whom you ask, of course, but, I believe the contemporary doctrine of eternal conscious torment in a place commonly called *hell*, was born out of the creative imaginations of theologians and storytellers who were trying to explain the unexplainable. The recipe for the fabrication of the contemporary notion of hell goes something like this: Start with the Old Testament Hebrew concept of *Sheol* (variously translated as the grave, death, the unknown beyond, the abode of the dead, the depths, e.g. Psalm 139:8). Next, mix in some Babylonian and Greco-Roman mythology by substituting the Greek word *Hades* for *Sheol* when translating the Old Testament from Hebrew to Greek. Then toss in some local Judean folklore about the Valley of Hinnom, or *Gehenna,* which had been the place where the wicked kings of Israel had offered human sacrifices to Molech and, by Jesus' day, had become the garbage dump of Jerusalem where fire was always burning and maggots devoured the rotting corpses of animals and indigents. Add some rabbinical object lessons using *Gehenna* as a word picture for what happens to the devil and "bad" people (as they defined them). Their teaching, as the disciples of Jesus reflected in their assumptions, was that the blind, deformed, lepers, and the mentally ill were that way because of some personal or familial sin (e.g. John 9:1). Blend these ingredients well, and then add the flavoring that came from Celtic and Anglo-Saxon mythologies when English translators put their spin on it. Allow it all to "bake" for a few centuries in the imagination of a very superstitious world occasionally basted by creative storytellers and preachers like Augustine or Dante.[1] Top it all off with a bunch of confusion about the meaning of the Greek words *aion* or *aionios* (most accurately translated as *an age* or *indeterminate amount of time*, but sometimes arbitrarily translated *eternal* for some uncertain reason by the King James translators),[2] and what you end up with is the horrible doctrine that a wrath-driven God sends everyone who doesn't believe what the church teaches about Jesus to be tormented in hell forever. Never has there been a scarier bogeyman lurking in the shadows of the imaginations of mystified children of God.

It is not my purpose here to develop all the historical, etymological, hermeneutical, and theological reasons for rejecting the doctrine of eternal damnation for humanity.[3] I simply want to point out there are other ways to understand hell within a biblical framework. It gives a much clearer understanding of the teachings of Jesus on the topic of hell when we recognize that most of his usage of *Gehenna* (the word most commonly translated as "hell" in the English translations of the Gospels) came in the context of contrasting the righteousness *he* taught with that taught by the Pharisees and teachers of the Law of his day (e.g., Matthew 5:21-22). In other words, Jesus took the metaphor commonly used by the Pharisees for God's judgment (that the city dumping grounds was a fitting end for everyone they classified as "sinners") and turned it back on them, teaching instead that, if anyone deserved "hell", it was the unmerciful and self-righteous among them, the Scribes and Pharisees. And, in every case Jesus employed the metaphor of *Gehenna* it had nothing to do with the necessity of having the "right" beliefs and confessions. As the parable of the sheep and goats (Matthew 25:31-46) points out, it's not the absence of a confession of faith in Christ, but the failure to live a charitable life that gets a *nation* cast into *"the eternal fire prepared for the Devil and his angels"*.

Yes, the Book of Revelation speaks apocalyptically of an *abyss* and *lake of fire*, but it is in the context of describing the ultimate overthrow of evil. It is an unwarranted leap, in my opinion, to assume the Revelator was describing the eternal destination of everyone who has not prayed a prayer of confession that they are a sinner and indicated their *decision* to accept Christ as their Savior.

Here's the point. We are sinners. Because we are sinners we sin. Sin leads to much sorrow (hell) if left to run its course. While we travail in the consequences of our sinful ways, the prospect of dying and facing what lies beyond the grave can be terrifying – especially when we haven't yet grasped how much God loves us and how committed he is to bring us into his reconciling grace. God has kept much of what lies beyond the grave hidden in his mystery. We do not like that, and in our spiritually insecure state have imagined wild, shadowy monsters. In an effort to face our fear that God and the Devil are out to get us, we have created "comfort blankets" of doctrines that presume to protect us from the bogeyman. But some things simply must be left in the realm of mystery and wonderment as we crawl into the "trailer" of God's unfailing and comforting promise, resting assured that in the end it will be "death", not us, that will be destroyed (I Corinthians 15:20-26).

14

A DISTANT LIGHT

"For the grace of God that brings salvation has appeared to all men. It teaches us to say "No" to ungodliness and worldly passions, and to live self-controlled, upright and godly lives in this present age, while we wait for the blessed hope— the glorious appearing of our great God and Savior, Jesus Christ, who gave himself for us to redeem us from all wickedness and to purify for himself a people that are his very own, eager to do what is good."
Titus 2:11-14

What do Mussolini, Hitler, various Roman Catholic popes, John F. Kennedy, Henry Kissinger, and former Soviet president Gorbachev all have in common? "End times" prognosticators at one time or another identified each of them as the antichrist.

Remember when there were eighty-eight reasons to believe that the Rapture was going to occur in 1988? Remember when many filled their bathtubs with water and stored up nonperishable food items because of the global meltdown anticipated by Y2K? Christian radio and television were overrun with "prophecy" teachers running around like Chicken Little declaring, "The sky is falling!" Some Christians live on a steady diet of doomsday scenarios like these. I already mentioned such a worldview was a prominent feature of my own growing-up years in that skewed form of Christianity I inherited.

It is easy to be a "Monday morning quarterback" and poke fun at this misguided mindset. But wait. If one truly believes that this planet is a lost cause and that getting off of it is one's only hope, then any distant "light" is going to seem worth pursuing. If the beady eyes of the Devil are all one can see reflected in the "headlights", certainly one will conclude, one of us doesn't belong here. If some are convinced that the Devil, along with his minions, and the earth and most of its inhabitants, are destined for immolation in a fiery hell, we shouldn't be too critical of their desire to venture off in quest of imagined escape. When one is gripped in fear and unable to recognize the safety at hand, one can only think about getting "off the mountain."

The anticipated return of Jesus Christ has been a hope for Christians since Jesus handed over his mission to his first disciples. It is a distant light that inspires hope. But there is only peril for those who think they can take a shortcut to get there. Vain attempts to hurry God's timetable by linking current headlines or notable political personalities with speculative, futuristic prophecy interpretations is little more than trying to take a shortcut to Christ's return. It also comes dangerously close to a blasphemous attempt to take control of matters that belong solely to God.

The timing and exact nature of Christ's return is one of the mysteries that remain closed behind God's "bedroom door". Jesus made that very clear to his disciples who were impatiently trying to hurry things up by speculating about their own future. *"When they met together, they asked him, "Lord, are you at this time going to restore the kingdom to Israel?"* (Acts 1:6). His answer was very direct. *"He said to them: 'It is not for you to know the times or dates the Father has set by his own authority. But you will receive power when the Holy Spirit comes on you; and you will be my witnesses in Jerusalem, and in all Judea and Samaria, and to the ends of the earth'"* (Acts 1:7-8). Jesus, in effect, restrained them from venturing off in that direction and coaxed them back into the "vehicle" of a safe and missional destiny. Like jumper cables to a stalled vehicle, the infusion of his power at Pentecost was to get them started on the road to tomorrow. "Take the good news to everyone," he instructed them. "Love God, love your neighbor as yourself, show everyone how much God loves them."

It is a good thing to want Jesus to return. I think we all join John the Revelator in praying, *"even so, come Lord Jesus"* (Revelation 22:20). Every sorrow, every ailment, every struggle, every reminder of our mortality makes us long all the more for the day when *" Jesus, who has been taken from you into heaven, will come back in the same way you have seen him go into heaven"* (Acts 1:11). It's just that it isn't for us to know when that will be. Nor, how it will take place.

One of the most embarrassing chapters of Christian history took place at the beginning of the 20th Century when Christians were swept up in a new interpretive scheme of wild speculations about the end times. This prophetic scheme became known as "Dispensationism". It had been proposed by John Nelson Darby and was popularized by C. I. Scoffield when his Bible study notes were incorporated into what became known as *The Scoffield Reference Bible,* which continues to be the preferred Bible in many churches.

In contrast to the understandable curiosity of Jesus' disciples who asked if Jesus' resurrection meant the messianic age had begun (Acts 1:6), the 'Darby Dispensationists' went hog-wild imagining end times scenarios that "proved" the imminence of the Rapture, the Great Tribulation with its antichrist, and the unleashing of God's pent up wrath toward unrepentant Israel. Since then, there has been an ever-changing list of world leaders who so-called "experts" and prophecy preachers are convinced will turn out to be *the* antichrist. Trying to predict whom it will be is important to dispensationists because they can then be on guard against being deceived by him in case the Rapture hasn't taken them away before he comes to power. Also, it means that the contemporaries of the antichrist are the "lucky ones" who get to be in the final countdown to the end.[1]

I remember well a guest prophecy teacher who stood in the pulpit of one of the most highly regarded conservative churches of my city in the early 1970's and demonstrated with his timelines and charts that there was no reason to expect the Rapture would be delayed beyond the late 1980's. He was predicting it would happen sooner than that. He actually suggested that some might want to borrow heavily to financially support ministries and then "let the antichrist pay for it," after the Christians are raptured. The service concluded with scores of people rushing to the altar of the church to make sure they were ready to meet Jesus. Many present that night returned to their cars after the service imagining what they might buy and leave the bill to be paid by those who were going to be left behind. How absurd!

The real tragedy of this false teaching is the "siege mentality" that has permeated much of the evangelical/ fundamental segment of Christ's church in recent history. Countless Christians have been duped into retreating into ecclesiastical "bunkers" to ride out the tough times they believe are foreshadowing the Devil's takeover of the planet just before their "great escape". It is one of the major contributing factors to the marginalization of many Christians in contemporary culture.

Some of the byproduct of this eschatology is a collective paranoia against anyone or anything that doesn't talk and act like "us". Since it is a foregone conclusion that the world has been written off by God and will be yielded to Satan's control, "true" Christians must be on guard against subversion by sinister worldly forces. Isolation and fear of "ungodly" outsiders flavor the behavior and conversation of these folks. For example, any suggestion of nations working together for world peace is especially onerous to them, because that is how the antichrist will take over the world, as they see it. Never mind that Jesus said, *"Blessed are the peacemakers."*

This doctrine contributes to one of the most deceptive and virile strains of anti-Semitism ever spawned. While on the surface many who hold to Dispensationism claim to be pro-Israel and pro-Jewish, their underlying anticipation is that, because most Jews won't "convert" to Christianity, God will focus his pent up wrath upon Israel in a "Great Tribulation" period that will follow (conveniently) the Church's removal from the scene in the Rapture. This coming Tribulation, which one so-called prophecy expert said would make Hitler's Holocaust look like a Sunday school picnic, will be deserved by Israel and the Jews, it is supposed, because they will have made a covenant with the antichrist instead of accepting Christ. Now, *that* is a demonically inspired teaching if there ever was one!

Dispensationism, as much as any other factor, causes some to become a shrill and hand wringing voice in the current political debate. Because they are expecting that evil is going to take over, they feel like they have to "hold the fort" until Jesus comes by defending their rights and values – even if they end up being on the side of bigotry and injustice in the process.

This doctrine has produced several generations of fear-ridden, paranoid Christians who are frustrated and mad at the world, and whose only hope for survival is leaving the planet. In the grip of angst and desperation, they hope to distance themselves from anyone they think might compromise their readiness while they stand outside heaven's door demanding to get in.

Fortunately, there is a consistent and growing body of biblical scholarship that debunks Darbyism. Hopefully, it will eventually be relegated to the trash heap of history with the countless other doctrines that have temporarily distracted Christians, have complicated the simplicity of the gospel, and have possibly slowed the advance of the kingdom of God.

Embrace with me the alternative that does not presume to understand things we are not intended to know, but rather, chases away the shadowy monsters of speculative and defeatist Dispensationism with Christ-centered hope and good news. It is the alternative that gives the cross of Christ its rightful place as the fully effective, *once for all*, remedy for sin. It unhesitatingly confesses that salvation is a gift of God's grace imparted to us solely upon the basis of faith in Christ, which also comes to us a gift of God. It upholds the veracity and character of God and worships him as *Abba*—our dear Heavenly Father. It is founded upon the premise that God is good, loving and merciful. It opens heaven and beckons all to come freely to the throne of grace. It affirms that God is our Heavenly Father, Jesus is Lord and Savior, and the Holy Spirit has been poured out upon all humanity. It is a view that expects God's kingdom to come and God's will to be done *on earth as it is in heaven*.[2] It is a view that genuinely believes that evil will be overcome by good, that mercy will triumph over judgment, that in his wrath God will never forget his mercy, and that nothing will separate us from God's love. It is a view that strongly believes that, "*Red and yellow, black and white, they are precious in his sight. Jesus loves the little children of the world."*

15

THE CONCLUSION IS INCLUSION

"And you also were included in Christ when you heard the word of truth, the gospel of your salvation. Having believed, you were marked in him with a seal, the promised Holy Spirit,"
— Ephesians 1:13

Exclusion is the lie of lies. The serpent in Eden used exclusion to drive a wedge between Adam, Eve and God by suggesting that God didn't want them to be like him. To hide from God (exclude God) was the first response of the fallen pair (Genesis 3). Adam tried to exclude himself from Eve by blaming her; Eve blamed the serpent. When Cain and Abel brought sacrifice to God, Cain sought to distinguish himself from Abel leading to bitter jealousy and murder.

In stark contrast to all of this is Jesus, of whom the Scripture says, *"He has broken down the wall of hostility that used to separate us"* (Ephesians 2:14). Elsewhere we are reminded that, *"There is neither Jew nor Greek, slave nor free, male nor female, for you are all one in Christ Jesus"* (Galatians 3:28). Jesus, the Prince of Peace, has undertaken the mission of removing everything that separates us from God and each other. In an all-encompassing and continuing expression of divine love and mercy, God is removing every vestige of the exclusionary lie. He is *"making everything new"* (Revelation 21:5) through Christ.

When Paul reminded the Ephesians they were *"included in Christ when* [they] *heard the word of truth, the gospel of* [their] *salvation"* (Ephesians 1:13), he was stressing that inclusion is the first component of the good news. When they heard that message, they had already been included in Christ—in his death, in his resurrection and in his glorification as the whole of Ephesians 1 indicates. When the Ephesians believed the good news that they were already included, they were given a guaranteeing deposit of their assured redemption—the indwelling Holy Spirit (1:14).

When the Scripture says, *"He is the atoning sacrifice for our sins, and not only for ours but also for the sins of the whole world"* (1 John 2:2), it is speaking of inclusion. When Paul wrote to the Galatians that he had been *"crucified with Christ,"* (as have we all, Galatians 2:20), he was writing about inclusion. When Ephesians 1:4 mentions we were *"chosen in* [Christ] *before the creation of the world..."* it is about inclusion. When Paul went on to tell the Ephesians in chapter 2 verse 6, *"And God raised us up with Christ and seated us with him in the heavenly realms..."* inclusion again. When I Corinthians 15:22 declares, *"For as in Adam all die, so in Christ will all be made alive"*, it is demonstrating inclusion.

Inclusion is the truth that sets us free. We are forever free to love God, free to love the human family, free to believe, free to hope, free to forgive, free to approach God. This is the good news God wants everyone to hear: *"That God was reconciling the world to himself in Christ, not counting men's sins against them"* (2 Corinthians 5:19). This is the good news that will overcome evil. This is the truth that empowers me to love my neighbor *and* my enemies. This is the message that releases me from judging and excluding others. With this powerful word settled in my heart I can trust God in every circumstance. I can believe the best for everybody. I don't have to hide from God anymore. Even when we realize we need discipline because of the sin that besets us all, we know God *"disciplines us for our good, that we may share in his holiness"* (Hebrews 12:10).

You may ask, is there anything God excludes? Of course there is. God excludes exclusion. In so doing he is in the process of removing from his creation such fruits of exclusion as condemnation, shame, bigotry, falsehood, pride, immorality, impurity, hatred, intolerance, selfish ambition, greed, debauchery, hypocrisy, uncharitableness, ignorance, poverty, injustice, sorrow, sickness and death. Toward that end, Hebrews 12:29 reminds us, *"God is a consuming fire,"* —a fire that touches everything we do. All evil, in whatever form it takes will not be able to survive the refining fire of God. Still, no matter how extensive the loss we suffer as God's *"fire* [tests] *the quality of each man's work... [Each one] will be saved, but only as one escaping through the flames"* (1 Corinthians 3:11-15). I do not think we are compelled to see this as a literal fire. It is a metaphor for purging, purifying and refining. As God completes the process of restoring all things (Acts 3:21), all the old rubbish left here by the first Adam (the unrighteous deeds of fallen humanity) will be burned up. Meanwhile, redeemed humanity is welcomed into the presence of God where eventually, *"He will wipe every tear from their eyes. There will be no more death or mourning or crying or pain, for the old order of things has passed away"* (Revelation 21:4).

Paul wrote about it in Romans 14:8-13: *"If we live, we live to the Lord; and if we die, we die to the Lord. So, whether we live or die, we belong to the Lord. For this very reason, Christ died and returned to life so that he might be the Lord of both the dead and the living. You, then, why do you judge your brother? Or why do you look down on your brother? For we will all stand before God's judgment seat. It is written: 'As surely as I live, says the Lord, every knee will bow before me; every tongue will confess to God.' So then, each of us will give an account of himself to God. Therefore let us stop passing judgment on one another. Instead, make up your mind not to put any stumbling block or obstacle in your brother's way."*

When we judge our brother we exclude. But when we realize we were *all* included in Christ and will *all* stand before him to give an account of our lives, there remains no compelling reason to judge and exclude. Free of any valid reason to exclude others, it follows that it is within our grasp to love our neighbors as ourselves. I, of course, am not implying that one need not have discernment in human relations. There is still a lot of evil out there and evil intentioned people do exist. We must be wise while refusing to judge anyone as our inferior, or being so arrogant as to think God prefers us to him or her. Be discerning, but don't presume to have some moral superiority over others. Not excluding means never allowing compassion and mercy to disappear from our attitudes and actions toward anyone.

When Christ-followers today rediscover the wonderful news that the world is now reconciled to God because of the efficacy of all that Jesus did in living, dying and living again, it will dramatically change the tone and content of our *message*. Rather than our message being one that says God loves you but will toss you into eternal conscious torment if you don't believe what we're telling you before you die, ours will be a message of simple good news. God loves you, accepts you, forgives you, believes in you, and counts you *now* as a member of his family for Jesus' sake. Period.

As we realize that the message of the cross is the powerful truth that sets everyone free, rather than our devoutness, acts of piety, church attendance and outward religious appearance, it will redefine our *mission*. Our mission is less about making converts, and more about simply allowing the good news to flavor our conversations as we go about our daily lives. Our mission isn't to go and build new and better religious institutions. It is to be salt and light in our homes, work places, schools and recreation. The love and light of Jesus in our own lives will influence others to follow our example and become Christ-followers, too.

As we realize how simple and fulfilling it is to experience the good news in our own lives, it will greatly alter our *motivations* for relating to others. We can love and accept people for who they are free of a pressure- producing agenda to get them to convert to our way of thinking and adopt our ways. God loved and gave. That's the only motive we are to have—love and give ourselves to others.

Simply loving God and loving people radically alters the *methods* we employ to practice our faith. Our methods will be less centered on church marketing strategies, resource depleting programs, religious professionals and specialized buildings to become more focused upon just giving of ourselves in a way that makes it a better world. It won't be so much about church sponsored religious duty, but more about, in the coming and going of our daily lives, feeding the hungry, refreshing the thirsty, opening our lives to strangers, clothing the poor and caring for the sick.

What I am advocating is an infinitely more relaxed and relational way to live. It is what I imagine Jesus had in mind when he told his followers that coming to him would provide us rest (Matthew 11:28). It's a more childlike approach to God that is not jaded by fear, mistrust, and a need to be in control; it's not willfully ignorant, but neither all stressed-out about the *mysteries* of God. It's bringing the "monsters" out of the closet and into the light of truth, knowing that things are going to be okay, no matter how unsettling they may seem in the moment, because God is good and loving and will never abandon us.

It is time for us to be mature enough to give up insecure worries that God might abandon and leave some of us behind. Let's appreciate as never before all that Christ accomplished via his life, crucifixion and resurrection. Let's believe Jesus' assurances that he came to seek and save what was lost—all of it! Let's believe God's heart for us is conciliatory, not retributional. Because of his indescribable and unsurpassed love, God has no need to deal with us from a human perspective, as our sins deserve. He has too grand a vision of redeemed humanity to get sidetracked into petty, punitive vengeance. His love will not fail.

Reading the Bible, taking time for worship (personal and corporate), daily reflection, and prayer are wonderful things to do—unless we find ourselves doing these things to *earn* something from God. It is a good thing to draw near to God. But, as Jesus tried to explain to his followers, it's best to do so as children—simply, unpretentiously, and knowing we're welcome.

With these things in mind, hear again the words of Jesus:

> *"God blesses those who realize their need for him,*
> *for the Kingdom of Heaven is given to them.*
> *God blesses those who mourn,*
> *for they will be comforted.*
> *God blesses those who are gentle and lowly,*
> *for the whole earth will belong to them.*
> *God blesses those who are hungry and thirsty for justice,*
> *for they will receive it in full.*
> *God blesses those who are merciful,*
> *for they will be shown mercy.*
> *God blesses those whose hearts are pure,*
> *for they will see God.*

God blesses those who work for peace,
for they will be called the children of God.
God blesses those who are persecuted because they live for
God, for the Kingdom of Heaven is theirs"
(Matthew 5:3-10 NLT).

APPENDIX

SO WHAT'S THE SOLUTION?

Here are some suggestions I would offer to get the Church back on course and, hopefully, avoid repeating the institutional mistakes of the past.

Let's relax about some of the mysteries of God and loosen our grip on inflexible biblical interpretations and doctrines that tend to put God in human made boxes. Think, study, pray, form opinions and share ideas, yes; but we must hold our opinions with an open hand and remain teachable. I agree with Pentecostal scholar Amos Yong whose "central thesis is that, because the Spirit of God is universally active in creation and new creation, 'the religions of the world, like everything else that exists, are providentially sustained by the Spirit of God for divine purposes'… that means Christians should be open to learning from and being enriched by the Spirit's work in world religions."[1] God's ways go beyond the confines of our tidy formulas and invite us to think outside of the box.

Let's put to rest the notion that it is the Christian's duty to 'fix' everybody else's thinking. People with differing views are not our enemies who must be conquered by 'apologetically armed' thought police. Instead, let us love, forgive and reach out to all who adhere to different, even threatening views—as God does. A love-nurtured relationship, not theological acumen and agreement, is the highest ideal. Loving our neighbors (and our enemies) as ourselves is Christ's intended mode of evangelism.

Try responding to everyone as if they are already included in Christ, abandoning terminology that divides and makes value judgments about others such as saved/unsaved, believer/unbeliever, churched/unchurched, Spirit-filled/not Spirit-filled and us/them. We can trust the Holy Spirit to "set the table" for inquiry and dialogue and then be ready to give an answer about our personal faith in Christ with gentleness and transparency when asked.

Put less emphasis upon church attendance numbers, church bank statements and real estate development as the measure of the progress of Christ's Church on earth. Instead, look for evidence of "redemptive lift" in a society; reduction in crime, social justice, reduced poverty, rising literacy, improved health, environmental enhancement, and expanding civility are the most reliable indicators of Christ's influence. Just because agencies other than local churches and denominations are also engaged in some of these social causes does not mean that their work and service in the community isn't a part of the advance of God's kingdom. *"Every good and perfect gift is from above, coming down from the Father of the heavenly lights,"* wrote James (1:17). If the evidence of redemptive lift seems to be lacking, opting to defend the turf of Christian institutions or posturing for political power isn't the answer, being the Church outside of the church is.

I'd like to see us all concentrating on cultivating healthy relationships in our spheres of influence (loving our neighbors). True spiritual and societal transformation happens one heart at a time as a loving community influences us, not because a particular group has been able to muscle its agenda onto the political center stage. We all are political in one form or another, and an informed and involved citizenry is essential to democracy; so I'm not an advocate of abandoning the political process. I do think however, that we should be loathe to label particular candidates and issues as "Christian", not because some candidates and issues aren't more in keeping with the cause of Christ, but because none of us are in a good position to *objectively* decide the matter. As we have learned from many scandals that have hit the headlines, we simply cannot know for sure what is going on in the private lives of others. And, on the American political scene at least, a "Christian" perspective is claimed and defended by opposing factions on virtually every issue. So let's prayerfully form our political views and participate in the debate, but avoid defending our positions from some presumed stance of superior piety.

Practice hospitality. In my view, this may be the single-most important step Christians can make toward taking the gospel of Jesus Christ into all the earth. Much has been written concerning the reality that the fast-paced, high stressed, materialistic lifestyle of today's "developed" nations has rendered hospitality as a lost art. Few families have the time or the resources, both economic and emotional, to open their hearts and homes to others for quality interaction. Too many of us have vectored our lives into orbit around high stress jobs, overloaded schedules, fast food, amusement, and exhaustion. Who has time for anything else? Thankfully, there is a rising tide of small group and home church expressions of Christianity that is a reaction to all this craziness and an advance toward simpler, more relational living. Those who *"practice hospitality"* as Romans 12:13 instructs, putting relationships ahead of religious busywork, will be key players in the new reformation that is underway.

FOOTNOTES

CHAPTER 1: GRANDPA

[1] The Rapture refers to what some believe will happen to a faithful minority just prior to the end of the world when they expect to be physically and suddenly taken up to be with Christ.

[2] The Marriage Supper of the Lamb is spoken of in Revelation 19:9. It is thought by some to be what the raptured ones will be enjoying in heaven, while the unbelievers and backslidden believers left behind on earth will be experiencing the unleashed wrath of God upon themselves and the planet in a final Tribulation period.

[3] I heard many sermons interpreting having an inadequate supply of oil for one's lamp from the parable of the Ten Virgins (Matthew 25:1-12) as symbolizing being unprepared for the Rapture.

CHAPTER 2: INSTITUTIONAL MAN

[1] John 16:12-13 clearly indicates that Jesus intentionally withheld some information from his disciples.

[2] Acts chapter one tells the story.

[3] Note that this sort of proof-texting and rolling of the dice is considered as an ill-advised way to seek spiritual guidance and make key leadership decisions today.

[4] *Apocalyptic* was a literary style common in biblical times that employed symbols such as the darkening of the sun or the moon turning to blood to indicate something of dramatic importance and change was underway.

[5] Peter quoted from Joel 2:28-30.

[6] *Canonical* is a word derived from *canon*, which was a measuring stick. In other words, writings were determined to be canonical if they measured up to certain standards set by church "authorities".

[7] See article, "The Road to Nicaea," *Christian History & Biography;* Issue 85 Winter 2005

[8] Ibid

[9] Ibid

[10] *Revolution,* George Barna, Tyndale House Publishing 2005

[11] See Appendix

CHAPTER 3: GOOD NEWS!

[1] These are little booklets that a person can quickly pull out of a pocket and share with someone to whom they are "witnessing." Each one, with slight variation, offers

scriptures to demonstrate that sinners are cut off from God because of their sin and only deserve to be punished. The sinner must admit he is a sinner in need of a Savior, and then make a "decision" to accept Christ as their personal Savior, and pray the sinner's prayer in order to be "born again".

[2] I Corinthians 9:16

[3] The word *gospel* means good news.

CHAPTER 4: THE B-I-B-L-E

[1] Miroslav Volf, of the Yale Divinity School Center for Faith and Culture, suggested, at a Theological Conversation jointly sponsored by Yale and Emergent, February 2006, that capital "T" Truth exists only in the mind of God. In contrast to the relativist who believes there is no absolute truth, Volf implied (if I understood him correctly) that absolute Truth does exist, but only God knows it fully. What we know to be truth should be considered small "t" truth.

[2] As Dawn Herzog Jewell reminds us in an article entitled *Winning the Oral Majority*, *Christianity Today*, March 2006, p. 56

CHAPTER FIVE: WHAT'S WRONG WITH THIS PICTURE?

[1] Quoting from *Universal Salvation? The Current Debate*, Edited by Robin A. Parry & Christopher H Partridge, Wm. B. Eerdmans Publishing Co., 2003, p. 248

[2] Genesis chapters 1-6 tell the story.

[3] LeRon Shults, formerly of Bethel Seminary, author and leading theologian, offered this thought on the Emergent-U.S. Web blog May 4, 2006: "Various communities throughout church history have often developed new creeds and confessions in order to express the Gospel in their cultural context, but the early modern use of linguistic formulations as 'statements' that allegedly capture the truth about God with certainty for all cultures and contexts is deeply problematic... Languages are culturally constructed symbol systems that enable humans to communicate by designating one finite reality in distinction from another. The truly infinite God of Christian faith is beyond all our linguistic grasping, as all the great theologians from Irenaeus to Calvin have insisted, and so the struggle to capture God in our finite propositional structures is nothing short of linguistic idolatry."

CHAPTER SIX: BLACK CAT

[1] I use the plural "them" in reference to God in the same sense that Genesis Chapter One uses the plural "us" in the English translation of *Elohim*– "Then God said, 'Let us make man in our image...'" (vs. 26). The reader should not conclude that I believe in three gods or anything other than the traditional Trinitarian understanding of one God.

[2] See *Exclusion & Embrace: A Theological Exploration of Identity, Otherness, and Reconciliation*, Miroslav Volf, Abingdon Press, 1996, for a very scholarly and insightful development of the idea of "embrace".

[3] Ephesians 1:6 King James Version

[4] The Scriptures (Romans 8:7) use the word *hostile* or *enmity* to describe our natural human posture toward God without Christ's intervention.

[5] *Abba* is the term of endearment similar to Papa or Daddy Jesus used when praying to his Heavenly Father.

[6] This familiar, but under appreciated portion of the Lord's Prayer (Matthew 6:10, Luke 11:2), clearly indicates where Jesus focused his prayers. Jesus wasn't envisioning a world written off by God and abandoned to the recycling bin of history. He envisioned and prayed for the invasion of (then underway) and inexorable advance of God's kingdom and will on earth.

[7] Some have adopted the tactic of employing the Old Covenant laws to biblically buttress certain political stances (e.g., support for the death penalty), while at the same time declaring, with Apostle Paul, that Christians have been set free from the Old Covenant law (Romans 8:1-4; Ephesians 2:15). It seems to me you can't have it both ways.

[8] Hebrews 5:8 speaking of Jesus states: *"Although he was a son, he learned obedience from what he suffered"*

CHAPTER 7: DISCIPLINE FOR THE "HELL" OF IT

[1] Even Sodom, the destruction of which is often cited as the model of God's wrath in action (Genesis 19), was later promised complete restoration by the prophet Ezekiel (Ezekiel 16-53-55).

[2] The technical term for this is the *Incarnation*—God taking on human form and walking the earth in the person of Jesus of Nazareth.

[3] Romans 12:19

[4] Some believe this discipline and refining continues post mortem, a view that is no more speculative than other theories and interpretations offered to explain mysteries such as what happens after we die, in my opinion.

[5] I Corinthians 13:8

[6] Romans 8:22

CHAPTER 8: MINISTERS

[1] Martin Luther was a German Roman Catholic monk who was troubled by abuses of power in the name of God and the church that were commonly practiced. He posted a document of protest on the door of the church in Wittenberg that is generally considered to be the starting point for what is known as the Protestant Reformation.

[2] Luther realized that, according to the Scriptures, we are made "just" (having right standing with God) by faith in Christ, rather than through religious works and purchased indulgences from a church official (Romans 1:17; Galatians 3:11).

[3] *The Crucible,* Arthur Miller, Bantam Books, 1959; with Introduction by Richard Watts, Jr., pp. 2-3

[4] 2004 Universal Studios

CHAPTER 9: CHURCH CONSUMERS

[1] I am troubled when businesses label themselves as "Christian" as if without the label a business isn't Christian. It's exclusive.

CHAPTER 10: HAZARDOUS MOBILITY

[1] Stanza from *Wand'ring Star*, hit song sung by Lee Marvin from the 1969 western musical film adaptation of *Paint Your Wagon*, a 1951 Broadway musical comedy, with book and lyrics by Alan J. Lerner and music by Frederick Loewe.

[2] Many Dispensationists interpret this parable to apply to a time after the Second Coming of Christ. I don't agree, but that's not my point here.

CHAPTER 11: I'VE BEEN WONDERING

[1] "Slain in the Spirit" is a phrase Pentecostals use to describe what happens when someone is so overwhelmed by a spiritual encounter that they are rendered unable to stand as when John wrote, upon seeing a vision of *"one like a son of man," "...I fell at his feet as though dead"* (Revelation 1:13, 17).

[2] This metaphor is taken from Genesis 11:4 where it records that the citizens of Babel said, *"Come, let us build ourselves a city, with a tower that reaches into the heavens..."*

CHAPTER 13: MONSTERS IN THE CLOSET

[1] Dante's *Inferno* is the source of much of our modern day perverted imagery of a literal hell.

[2] This word study alone, which most adherents to a literal hell doctrine have never done, is sufficient to raise serious doubts about some of the commonly accepted notions about hell.

[3] See *http://www.what-the-hell-is-hell.com/teeth.htm* for an in depth analysis and presentation of scholarship on the topic. Also, *The Last Word and the Word After That,* Brian

D. McLaren, Jossey-Bass, 2005 provides much food for thought.

CHAPTER 14: A DISTANT LIGHT

[1] I am amused by the story of the seminary professor who said he was having a great day until he learned that his choice for antichrist had died.

[2] Brian D. McLaren, in his book *The Secret Message of Jesus*, W Publishing Group, 2006, has made a wonderful contribution toward understanding what Jesus meant when he spoke of the kingdom of God.

APPENDIX

[1] As characterized by Roger E. Olson in an article entitled "A Wind that Swirls Everywhere", *Christianity Today*, March 2006, pp. 53-54.

Printed in the United States
84603LV00002B/75/A